Peaceful Plant-Eating Dinosaurs

THE DINOSAUR LIBRARY

Peaceful Plant-Eating Dinosaurs
The Iguanodonts, Duckbills, and Other Ornithopods

Thom Holmes and Laurie Holmes
Illustrated by Michael William Skrepnick

Series Advisor:
Dr. Peter Dodson
Professor of Veterinary Anatomy and Paleontology,
University of Pennsylvania
and
co-editor of *The Dinosauria*,
the leading reference used by dinosaur scientists

Enslow Publishers, Inc.

40 Industrial Road   PO Box 38
Box 398   Aldershot
Berkeley Heights, NJ 07922 Hants GU12 6BP
USA   UK

http://www.enslow.com

Library of Congress Cataloging-in-Publication Data

Holmes, Thom.
    Peaceful plant-eating dinosaurs : the iguanodonts, duckbills, and other
ornithopods/ Thom Holmes and Laurie Holmes ; illustrated by Michael William
Skrepnick.
        p. cm. — (The dinosaur library)
    Includes bibliographical references (p.) and index.
    ISBN 0-7660-1450-9
    1. Ornithischia—Juvenile literature. [1. Dinosaurs. 2. Herbivores, Fossil.]
I. Holmes, Laurie. II. Skrepnick, Michael William, ill. III. Title. IV. Title:
Iguanodonts, duckbills, and other ornithopod dinosaurs. V. Series: Holmes, Thom.
Dinosaur library.
    QE862.O65H66   2001
    567.914—dc21

                                        00-010020

Printed in the United States of America

10 9 8 7 6 5 4 3 2

To Our Readers: We have done our best to make sure all Internet addresses in this book were
active and appropriate when we went to press. However, the author and the publisher have
no control over and assume no liability for the material available on those Internet sites or on
other Web sites they may link to. Any comments or suggestions can be sent by e-mail to
comments@enslow.com or to the address on the back cover.

Illustration Credits: Michael William Skrepnick. Illustrations on p. 48 after
Charig/Crompton, 1962 (*Heterodontosaurus*), after Galton, 1974a (*Hypsilophodon*),
after Gilmore, 1909 (*Camptosaurus*); p. 49 after Janensch, 1955 (*Dryosaurus*), after
Norman, 1980 (*Iguanodon*), after Weishampel, 1981b (*Corythosaurus*); p. 50 after
Lambe, 1920.

Photo Credits: © Corel Corporation, pp. 9, 17, 73; © Digital Vision, Ltd., p. 32;
Wayne Grady, p. 6 (Thom Holmes); Shaina Holmes, p. 6 (Laurie Holmes); Thom
Holmes, pp. 25, 42, 45, 47 (taken at the American Museum of Natural History),
93, 97; Michael Tropea, p. 7.

Cover Illustration: Michael William Skrepnick

Contents

About the Authors

Thom Holmes is a natural history writer specializing in dinosaur science. He has dug for dinosaurs with leading paleontologists in the United States and South America. He has collaborated with Dr. Peter Dodson on several dinosaur-related projects during the past fifteen years.

Laurie Holmes is a science writer and editor, as well as a reading specialist. It has been her privilege to associate with many of the world's leading dinosaur scientists and artists through her work with her husband, Thom. Originally a teacher, she maintains that she is still teaching by writing and editing books for young adults.

On a dig in Patagonia, Thom Holmes holds part of the skull bone of what is currently known as the largest meat-eating dinosaur ever.

Thom Holmes

Laurie Holmes

Authors' Note

Dinosaurs hold a special fascination for people all over the world. In writing *The Dinosaur Library*, we enjoyed sharing the knowledge that allows scientists to understand what dinosaurs were really like. You will learn about the differences that make groups of dinosaurs unique, as well as the many similarities that dinosaurs shared.

The Dinosaur Library covers all the suborders of dinosaurs, from the meat-eating theropods, such as *Tyrannosaurus rex*, to the gigantic plant eaters. We hope you enjoy learning about these fascinating creatures that ruled the earth for 160 million years.

ABOUT THE ILLUSTRATOR

Michael William Skrepnick is an established paleo artist with a lifelong interest in dinosaurs. He has worked on newly described dinosaurs with a number of the world's leading paleontologists. His original artworks are found in a number of art collections and reproduced as museum murals, and in popular books, magazines, scientific journals, and television documentaries.

Michael lives and works in Alberta, Canada, close to some of the richest Upper Cretaceous dinosaur fossil localities in the world.

Paleo art is a field devoted to the reconstruction and life restoration of long extinct animals and their environments. Since we cannot observe dinosaurs (other than living birds) in nature, we may never truly know their habits, lifestyles, or the color of their skin. In addition, the fossil record provides only a fraction of the remains of a wide diversity of life on earth.

Many fairly complete skeletons of dinosaurs have been unearthed in recent history. Others are represented by as little as a fragment of a single fractured bone, an isolated tooth, or a footprint impressed in once-wet mud. It is still possible to create a reliable portrait of unique, previously unknown creatures, but the accuracy of the art depends on the following:

- The quality and amount of actual skeletal material of the specimen preserved
- Discussion and collaboration with a paleontologist familiar with the fossil material and locality from which it was excavated
- Observation and comparisons to the closest related living forms
- The technical abilities, skill, and disciplined vision of the artist

The resulting artwork can draw the viewer back in time into exotic worlds of the ancient.

THE NESTING GROUND

*T*he herd of Maiasaura *had been traveling for several weeks to reach its destination. Migrating from the north, the group was several thousand strong. Along the way the animals had stopped to eat once or twice each day on the vegetation that lined both sides of the trail. They journeyed through vast evergreen forests, where the food was tough and dry. They ate the needles, bark, and cones of pine trees; occasionally fronds from cycads; and ferns that blanketed the forest bed.*

As they traveled south on their annual migration, the vegetation became more lush and abundant. Flowering shrubs were beginning to bloom. Many had berries and soft branches with leaves. The air was warm and humid. Nature was bursting with life all around the hadrosaurs.

Ahead of the herd lay a vast coastal plain. It was a wide expanse of land that slowly rose from an inland sea about a hundred miles away. The land closer to the sea flooded frequently. It was not a good place for hadrosaurs to build their nests. The eggs would rot or become buried by flash floods, which were common during the spring. Instead, the herd headed for a higher part of the plain about halfway between the inland sea and the mountains. There the vegetation was firmly rooted and grew rapidly. This was the place where the animals would build nests and lay their eggs. The greenery that covered the plain included patches of shrubs, trees, and ground cover that would feed the hungry hadrosaurs and their young for many months.

Among the herd were yearlings from the previous year's nesting season. They were still too young to mate and lay eggs. Being nearly full grown, however, they were able to keep up with the larger, 30-foot- (9-meter-) long adults in the herd. The yearlings were playful; they darted among the giant adults, nipping at each other's tails.

Along their journey, the maiasaur herd had been followed by several large predators. The meat eaters kept their distance, mostly traveling along the outskirts of the herd, waiting for the sick and older members of the group to become separated from the rest. They would then dispose of them with ease. The carnivores knew that this was less risky than entering the herd, where the larger duckbills could hurt them with their tremendous weight. As the duckbills reached the area that would become their nesting ground, they noticed that the big meat eaters had disappeared. But they could still sense that danger lurked nearby.

The entire herd seemed to know that it had reached its traditional nesting ground. Many of the duckbills quietly groaned and honked as they arrived at familiar territory.

The adult females spread out from the herd onto the plain,

looking for good nesting sites. When they picked a spot, they were careful not to crowd one another. Each took up just enough space so that she could turn around in a circle and not rub against a neighbor. Once they staked their claim, the nest building began.

The ground was still moist and soft from an overnight rain. The earthy smell of the soil was familiar to members of the herd that had been there before.

Some of the yearlings watched as one of the adult females began to make a nest. First she used her hind legs and large padded feet to scoop up a pile of mud, making a mound. She then used her hands to shape a hole in the middle of the mound. It was about 6 feet (1.8 meters) across and 2 to 3 feet (almost 1 meter) deep. This would soon be the home for her eggs. Other female hadrosaurs all across the plain were making similar nests.

Soon after they completed the nests, the females mated. Then, each mother laid between fifteen and twenty oval-shaped eggs in the pit within each mound. The eggs were not laid in any particular pattern, but they were stuck in the mud so that they stood up on end. After laying their eggs, the duckbills gathered loose vegetation in their mouths from the surrounding area. They placed the plants on top of the eggs to keep them warm, which would help them incubate.

The females tended their nests by resting alongside them. They would walk off to get food every now and then, but they did so with caution. Within the nesting grounds, they were relatively safe from large predators. The large meat eaters did not tangle with groups of adult hadrosaurs. Instead, they waited just outside the

perimeter of the nesting ground, ready to ambush any unsuspecting duckbill that strayed into their space.

The females were also cautious about leaving their nests unattended. Packs of the small meat eater Troodon roamed the outskirts of the camp. They would sneak into the nesting site and steal eggs for supper.

One day the tiny squeaking of baby duckbills could be heard in different corners of the nesting site. The hatchlings were less than 2 feet (60 centimeters) long. Day by day, the sound of hatching babies increased until the entire nesting site was alive with the noise of newborn dinosaurs.

The job of tending their babies fully occupied the mother

duckbills. When duckbills hatched, they could not fend for themselves. They would remain in the nest for many months, growing to more than 3 feet (1 meter) long before they would be able to walk on their own. During this time, their mother would bring them food and try to protect them from danger. The teeth of the babies were already formed, and they could chew even the toughest plants. Although berries and the succulent leaves of flowering plants were the best foods to help them grow fast, the mother duckbills soon found these kinds of plants in short supply. Day by day, they had to go a little farther to get food for their young. When the softer plants were not available, they picked ferns and the twigs of pine trees in their mouths and carried them back to the nest.

The nesting grounds attracted large numbers of Troodons. As the mother hadrosaurs wandered farther and farther to get food for their young, they left their nests unattended for longer and longer periods. The Troodons became bold in their raids on the nests. The predators would race into the nesting site, listen for the squeaking babies, and step into the first unprotected nest they could find. There they would snatch up a baby hadrosaur in their teeth or hands and race away before the mother duckbill returned. Sometimes a large male Maiasaura would scare a Troodon away. The yearlings, too, helped by staying close to untended nests. But the nesting area was noisy and lively and full of activity, making it easier for the Troodon to prey on the young without being noticed. The Troodon were not always lucky, however. All it took was the quick stomp of a mother Maiasaura or the rapid swipe of its heavy tail to smash one of the delicate meat eaters into lifelessness.

After about eight or nine months, the Maiasaura young were ready to leave the nest and face the world. They had grown rapidly and were now able to walk and run with ease. Stepping out from under the shadow of their great mother was exciting but frightening. As many as half of the babies had already died of sickness or had been carried off by raiding meat eaters. The others had to learn to survive in the wide-open world. This would begin, as the story had begun for their parents many years before, with a journey. The herd gathered together with a quiet thunder that shook the earth as the animals walked. They completed the cycle of their migration by heading back north.

Author's Note—The preceding dinosaur story is fiction but is based on scientific evidence and ideas suggested by paleontologists. You will find explanations to support these ideas in the chapters that follow. Use the following guide to find these references:

- Herding and migration: pages 73, 87 (Eggs and Babies, Ornithopod Defenses)
- Vocalizing and senses: page 57 (Physiology)
- Nest making and parental care: page 73 (Eggs and Babies)
- Chewing and eating: page 44 (Ornithopod Skulls and Teeth)
- Diet: page 79 (Feeding Habits and Adaptations)
- Defenses: page 87 (Ornithopod Defenses)

CHAPTER 1

DINOSAURS DEFINED

What are dinosaurs? They were reptiles, but they were a special kind that no longer exists. Many people assume that all dinosaurs were gigantic. Some confuse the dinosaurs with extinct reptiles that flew (the pterosaurs) and those that lived in the sea (e.g., plesiosaurs, ichthyosaurs, and mosasaurs). How does one know for sure whether a creature was a dinosaur or not?

Dinosaurs came in many shapes and sizes. Some were many times larger than the largest land animals alive today. Others were as small as chickens. Some were carnivores (they ate meat); others were herbivores (they ate mostly plants). Some walked on two legs, others on four legs. Yet, in spite of these vast differences, vertebrate paleontologists who study dinosaurs have identified many specific characteristics that allow them to classify dinosaurs as a group of related creatures, different from all others.

Dinosaurs lived only during the Mesozoic Era. The age of dinosaurs spanned from the Late Triassic Period, about 225 million years ago, to the Late Cretaceous Period, some 65 million years ago. Fossils dating from before or after that time were not dinosaurs. This rule also means that all dinosaurs are *extinct.* Today's birds, however, are believed to be modern relatives of the dinosaurs.

Dinosaurs were a special kind of reptile. Dinosaurs had basic characteristics common to all reptiles. They had a backbone and scaly skin, and they laid eggs. Meat-eating dinosaurs are believed to have been the ancestors of birds, with some showing birdlike features such as clawed feet, hollow bones, and even feathers.

Dinosaurs were land animals. Reptiles that flew in the air or lived in the water were around at the same time as dinosaurs, but they were *not* dinosaurs. Dinosaurs were built to walk and live on land only, although they may have occasionally waded in the water.

Dinosaurs had special skeletal features. Dinosaurs walked differently than other reptiles because of their hips. Dinosaurs had either ornithischian (birdlike) hips or saurischian (lizardlike) hips. Both kinds of hips allowed dinosaurs to walk with their legs tucked under their bodies to support their full weight. This mammal- or birdlike stance is clearly different from the sprawling stance of today's reptiles. A dinosaur would never have dragged its stomach along the ground like a crocodile or lizard. Other distinguishing skeletal features of dinosaurs include:

- Three or more vertebrae (backbones) attaching the spine to the hip.

- A ball-and-socket joint attaching the legs to the hip for increased mobility and flexibility.

- High ankles and long foot bones. (Dinosaurs walked on their toes.)

- A simple hinge joint at the ankle.

- Three or fewer finger bones on the fourth finger of each forefoot (hand) or no fourth finger at all.

- Three to five clawed or hoofed toes on the hind limb (foot).

Understanding Dinosaurs

The study of extinct fossil organisms is called paleontology. *Paleo* means "ancient." Paleontologists use fossil traces of ancient organisms as a window onto life in the distant past, before the evolution of modern man.

Most of what we know about dinosaurs comes from our knowledge of their fossilized skeletons and the layers of earth in which they are found. Putting a dinosaur together is like doing a jigsaw puzzle without a picture to follow. Fortunately, because dinosaurs were vertebrates, all dinosaur skeletons are similar in some ways. A basic knowledge of vertebrate skeletons, and of dinosaur skeletons in particular, helps guide the paleontologist in putting together a new fossil jigsaw puzzle.

While no human being has ever seen a dinosaur in the flesh, much can be revealed by studying the fossil clues. The paleontologist must have a firm grasp of scientific methods

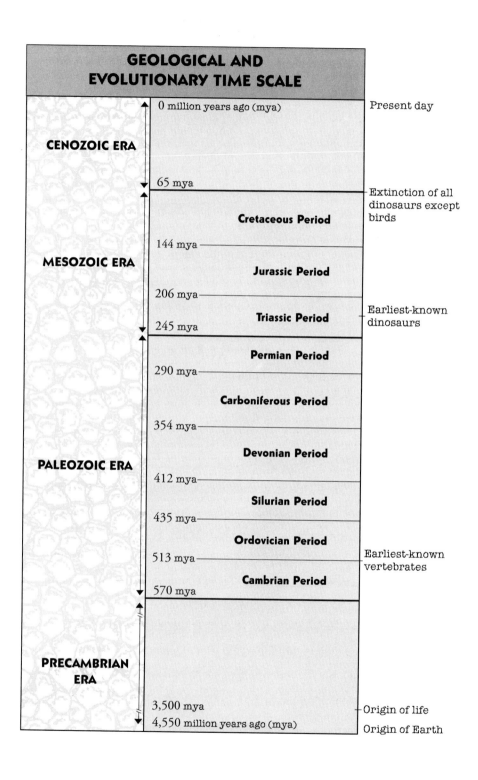

GEOLOGICAL AND EVOLUTIONARY TIME SCALE

0 million years ago (mya) — Present day

CENOZOIC ERA

65 mya — Extinction of all dinosaurs except birds

MESOZOIC ERA

Cretaceous Period

144 mya

Jurassic Period

206 mya

Triassic Period — Earliest-known dinosaurs

245 mya

PALEOZOIC ERA

Permian Period

290 mya

Carboniferous Period

354 mya

Devonian Period

412 mya

Silurian Period

435 mya

Ordovician Period

513 mya — Earliest-known vertebrates

Cambrian Period

570 mya

PRECAMBRIAN ERA

3,500 mya — Origin of life

4,550 million years ago (mya) — Origin of Earth

and fact. He or she must also have imagination and a knack for solving mysteries. Fossils provide evidence for the construction of dinosaurs. The paleontologist examines these facts and tries to understand how they affected the lifestyle and behavior of the dinosaurs.

Our knowledge of dinosaurs grows every year. This book, and others in the series, will help you understand the many kinds of dinosaurs and how they lived. It is based on the latest scientific evidence and shows us that dinosaur science is alive and well all around the world. After all, if scientific estimates are correct, there may have been as many as 1,200 unique kinds, or genera, of dinosaurs, only about 350 of which have yet been discovered.[1] If you decide to make a career out of dinosaur science, maybe one day you will add a new dinosaur or two to the list.

The Ornithopods

The ornithopods were a plentiful group of two-legged plant eaters that thrived during most of the age of dinosaurs. They filled a place in nature that is today occupied by cattle, moose, horses, antelope, and other peaceable plant eaters that provide a steady supply of food for predators. Ornithopods were the most successful and widespread of all herbivorous dinosaurs of the Cretaceous Period. There is evidence that they traveled in great herds, nested in large colonies to lay their eggs, and took care of their young until their offspring were large enough to fend for themselves. Ornithopods first walked the earth in the Early Jurassic Period, not long after the appearance of the earliest dinosaurs. The last of the great ornithopods disappeared at the end of the age of dinosaurs, along with *Tyrannosaurus* ("tyrant lizard") and the horned dinosaurs.

The term *ornithopod* is short for Ornithopoda ("bird-footed"), a suborder of ornithischian dinosaurs. Ornithopoda includes several kinds of well-known dinosaurs, such as *Iguanodon* ("iguana tooth"), one of the earliest dinosaurs ever described, and the hadrosaur or "duck-billed" dinosaurs, so named because their spoonlike mouth resembled that of a duck. Unlike some other plant-eating dinosaurs that had armor and horns, ornithopods had few special defenses. They ranged in length from about 4 feet (just over 1 meter) in *Heterodontosaurus* ("different-toothed lizard") to about 49 feet (15 meters) for the duck-billed *Shantungosaurus* ("Shantung lizard").

Only about 18 percent of all the individual kinds, or genera, of dinosaurs recognized so far are ornithopods. This figure may seem low, but one must keep in mind that ornithopods existed in greater numbers than most other kinds of dinosaurs. The fossil record of

The plant-eating *Iguanodon* was the first dinosaur ever described.

ornithopods is good. Many are known from nearly complete skeletons or multiple specimens, as opposed to the fragments of evidence for many kinds of sauropods (another type of plant-eating dinosaurs) and theropods (meat-eating dinosaurs). So, although we may be able to name a larger number of different kinds of meat-eating dinosaurs, the ornithopods and other plant eaters on which the theropods fed must have greatly outnumbered them.

Six families of ornithopods evolved during the age of dinosaurs. They appeared in roughly the following order:

206 mya (million years ago)			144 mya		65 mya
Early Jurassic	Middle Jurassic	Late Jurassic	Early Cretaceous		Late Cretaceous

Heterodontosaurs

Hypsilophodonts

Dryosaurs

Camptosaurs

Iguanodonts

Hadrosaurs

There is an abundance of fossil evidence for ornithopods. It has told us everything from how their skin must have looked to how they raised their young and how some could trumpet sounds through fancy head crests. Because of their plentiful fossils, scientists probably understand the lifestyle of the ornithopods better than that of any other dinosaurs.

CHAPTER 2

ORIGINS AND EVOLUTION

When the first dinosaurs evolved, they were part of a rich biological history that had already spanned hundreds of millions of years. Dinosaurs descended from land vertebrates. Land vertebrates descended from ocean vertebrates, which began wandering onto land about 370 million years ago. All of these early animals lived at least part of their lives in the water. Even today's amphibians, which take to the land as adults, begin as waterborne creatures. Adult amphibians still need to return to the water to lay their eggs.

The most important biological event leading to true land animals was the evolution of the amniotes, vertebrate animals that could fertilize their eggs internally. These included reptiles and birds, which laid shelled eggs on land, and mammals, whose fertilized eggs developed within their bodies. Humans, birds, lizards, snakes, turtles, and even dinosaurs are all related by being amniotes.

Dinosaurs fall within the class of vertebrates known as

Reptilia, or reptiles. Reptiles are egg-laying backboned animals with scaly skin. The different kinds of reptiles, living and extinct, are grouped by certain features of their skeletons. Most important is the design of the reptilian skull. Dinosaurs fall within the subclass Diapsida, which includes reptiles whose skulls had a pair of openings behind each eye. Diapsida is divided into two groups: the lepidosaurs and the archosaurs. Lepidosaurs consist of the kinds of lizards and snakes that live today. Archosaurs consist of the thecodonts, a group of reptiles from the Triassic Period, some of which were small meat eaters that had begun to run on two feet; the crocodiles (living and extinct); the pterosaurs (extinct flying reptiles); and the dinosaurs.[1] All dinosaurs are probably descendants of a single common archosaurian ancestor.[2]

The dinosaurs and other diapsid reptiles were some of the most successful land vertebrates of all time. Dinosaurs first appeared about 225 million years ago and began to spread rapidly by the end of the Triassic Period.[3] Figure 1 summarizes the evolution of vertebrates leading to the dinosaurs and their bird descendants.

Dinosaur Beginnings

The archosaurs included a variety of reptiles of many sizes, some of which led to the dinosaurs. Some evolved with four sprawling legs, while others gradually began to walk or sprint for short distances on their two hind legs. By the Late Triassic Period, about 225 million years ago, some two-legged meat-eating creatures had evolved specialized hips and legs to help

Vertebrate Origins and Evolution
Leading to Dinosaurs

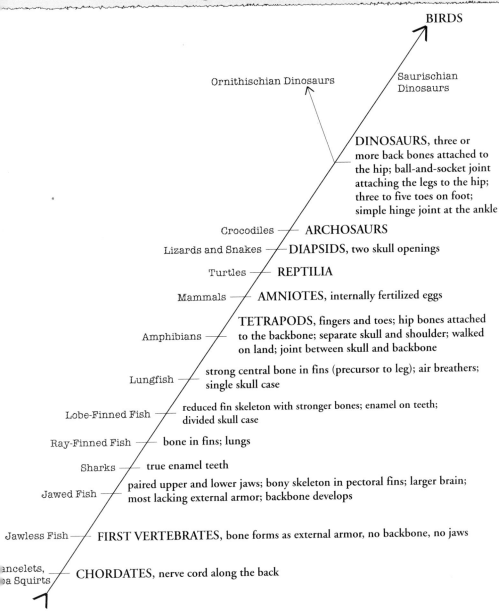

BIRDS

Ornithischian Dinosaurs

Saurischian
Dinosaurs

DINOSAURS, three or
more back bones attached to
the hip; ball-and-socket joint
attaching the legs to the hip;
three to five toes on foot;
simple hinge joint at the ankle

Crocodiles —— ARCHOSAURS

Lizards and Snakes —— DIAPSIDS, two skull openings

Turtles —— REPTILIA

Mammals —— AMNIOTES, internally fertilized eggs

TETRAPODS, fingers and toes; hip bones attached
to the backbone; separate skull and shoulder; walked
on land; joint between skull and backbone

Amphibians ——

strong central bone in fins (precursor to leg); air breathers;
single skull case

Lungfish ——

reduced fin skeleton with stronger bones; enamel on teeth;
divided skull case

Lobe-Finned Fish ——

Ray-Finned Fish —— bone in fins; lungs

Sharks —— true enamel teeth

paired upper and lower jaws; bony skeleton in pectoral fins; larger brain;
most lacking external armor; backbone develops

Jawed Fish ——

Jawless Fish —— FIRST VERTEBRATES, bone forms as external armor, no backbone, no jaws

ancelets,
ea Squirts —— CHORDATES, nerve cord along the back

Figure 1. This diagram shows how vertebrate animals evolved to yield dinosaurs.
The steps along the way include evolutionary changes that are directly related
to the traits of dinosaurs. The time span from the appearance of the first chordates to the last dinosaur (not including birds) is about 460 million years.

them stand erect. This supported the full weight of their bodies while they walked on two feet. They ranged in size from about 6 inches (15 centimeters) to 13 feet (4 meters). These kinds of archosaurs led to the first dinosaurs.

By the Late Triassic Period, two distinct branches of dinosaurs had evolved based on their hip designs. The saurischians included the carnivorous theropods and herbivorous sauropods. The ornithischians included the remaining assortment of plant eaters, such as ornithopods (duckbills, iguanodonts, and others) and armored and horned dinosaurs.

Ornithopods first appeared in the Early Jurassic Period, about 200 million years ago. This was soon after the first meat eaters and early kinds of long-necked plant-eating sauropods. The first ornithopods were heterodontosaurs, small plant eaters that were only about 3 to 4 feet (1 meter) long. They lived in the shadow of larger carnivores and herbivores. From these humble beginnings evolved a wide assortment of ornithopods large and small. They eventually spread throughout the world.

The Ornithopod Groups

Dinosaurs in the group called ornithopods were quite different in many ways. Some snorted through elaborate hollow crests on their heads. Others had protruding front teeth and small tusks. Still others had spikes for thumbs, and many were equipped with an unimaginable number of teeth for grinding food. Still, they all shared several common characteristics that separated them from other kinds of dinosaurs.

Ornithopods were among the first dinosaurs with ornithischian hips, one of the two kinds of hips found in dinosaurs. They were all herbivores. They walked primarily on two legs, although many could lean forward on strong front legs to walk on all fours at times. The term *ornithopod* means "bird foot." Except for the fact that they all had three weight-bearing toes, the design of ornithopod feet varied considerably. Some, including *Hypsilophodon* and *Tenontosaurus*, had sharp claws. Iguanodonts had blunt claws, and the feet of the hadrosaurs were bulky and thickly padded. Finally, ornithopods had a number of less obvious things in common, including features of their teeth and jaws. There was no hole in the outside of the lower jaw like other ornithischians, and beginning with the iguanodonts, the pubic bone on their hip jutted strongly forward.

Many of the ornithopods are well known from abundant fossil specimens. This has helped paleontologists firmly define the family tree of these dinosaurs. It can clearly be seen that duck-billed dinosaurs were descended from iguanodonts and that iguanodonts bear a close kinship to the camptosaurs before them. The earliest ornithopods—the heterodontosaurs and hypsilophodonts—eventually split off to become quite different from the others, but they still served as the starting point from which the other ornithopods evolved.

It is easiest to distinguish between one kind of ornithopod and another by understanding the different groups to which they belonged. The following chart is a summary of ornithopod families organized chronologically by known specimens.

Heterodontosaurs ("different-toothed lizards")

Turkey-sized early and primitive ornithopods. They were notable for their variety of teeth; small tusklike canine teeth on the upper and lower jaws, flat grinding teeth in the rear, and plucking teeth in the top front part of the jaw.

Time: Early Jurassic to Late Jurassic
Period

Abrictosauru

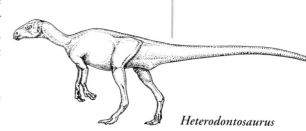

Heterodontosaurus

Hypsilophodonts ("high-crested tooth")

Ranging in size from that of a medium to large dog, these ornithopods had a simple single row of teeth, a beak, long arms, sharp claws, and a small head with large eyes.

Time: Middle Jurassic to Late
Cretaceous Period

Notohypsilophodon
Orodromeus, Othnielia
Parksosaurus, Yandusauru

Hypsilophodon

Dryosaurs ("oak lizards")

Lightly built ornithopods with a narrow snout, short arms, and long, slender legs for running fast. Measuring between 9 and 21 feet (2.7 to 6.4 meters) in length.

Time: Late Jurassic to Early
Cretaceous Period

Valdosaurus

Dryosaurus

ORNITHOPOD FAMILIES	SOME MEMBERS

Camptosaurs ("bent lizards")

Callovosaurus

Ranging from about 4 feet (1.2 meters) to 23 feet (7 meters) in length, they had a bulky body, short arms, and a stout head. Similar to iguanodonts, which followed them.

Time: Late Jurassic to Early Cretaceous Period

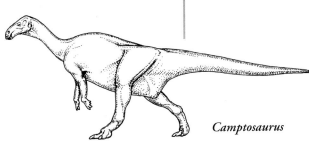

Camptosaurus

Iguanodonts ("iguana tooth")

Altirhinus, Lurdusaurus, Ouranosaurus,

Bulky and large, up to 30 feet (9 meters) in length, with a broad, toothless beak backed up by a sturdy set of grinding teeth and a prominent thumb spike on each hand.

Time: Early Cretaceous Period

Iguanodon

Hadrosaurs ("bulky lizards")

Edmontosaurus, Hadrosaurus, Lambeosaurus, Maiasaura, Parasaurolophus

The last and largest of the ornithopods to evolve. The largest measured about 49 feet (15 meters) in length. They had bulky bodies, stout arms, long flat beaks, and hundreds of grinding teeth. Many had hollow head crests.

Time: Late Cretaceous Period

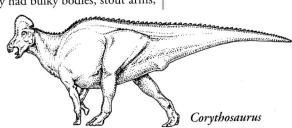

Corythosaurus

ome ornithopods are still not understood well enough to place them in these groups. These include such inosaurs as *Tenontosaurus* and *Muttaburrasaurus*, among others.

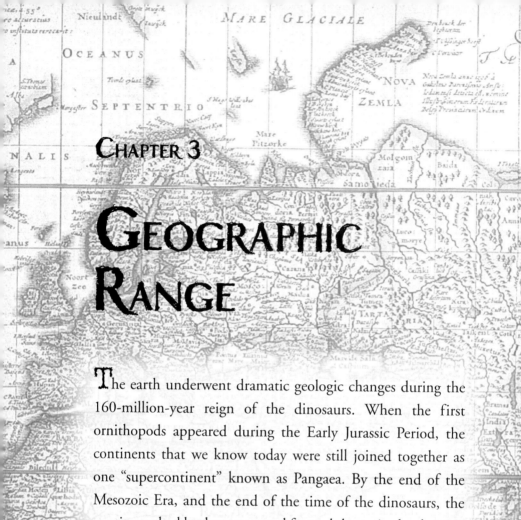

Chapter 3

Geographic Range

The earth underwent dramatic geologic changes during the 160-million-year reign of the dinosaurs. When the first ornithopods appeared during the Early Jurassic Period, the continents that we know today were still joined together as one "supercontinent" known as Pangaea. By the end of the Mesozoic Era, and the end of the time of the dinosaurs, the continents had broken apart and formed the major landmasses known today as North and South America, Africa, Europe, Asia, Australia, and Antarctica.

When the continents were joined, it was possible for dinosaurs to travel across the dry land. The theropods and prosauropods, the earliest known dinosaurs, spread rapidly around the globe while the continents were still connected. The ornithopods came a little later and spread slowly until the Cretaceous Period approached. During the Early and Late Cretaceous Periods, when the northern and southern continents had already separated, the number of iguanodonts and duck-billed dinosaurs exploded. These successful ornithopods lived mostly in North America, Europe, and Asia. Ornithopods are rarely found in South America, Africa, or Australia.

TRIASSIC

North America was connected to Europe and Asia by a land bridge during the Early and Late Cretaceous Periods. This accounts for similarities between duck-billed dinosaurs from China and North America.

EARLY JURASSIC

As the continents continued to separate, it became harder for the dinosaurs to spread to different areas. Today's arrangement of the continents was almost formed by the end of the Cretaceous Period, the end of the dinosaur era.

The greatest concentrations of ornithopod fossils have been

EARLY CRETACEOUS

Ornithopod Fossil Locations Around the World

found in the northwestern regions of North America, western Europe, and China. Iguanodonts have been found mostly in England and Europe. The largest duck-billed dinosaur, *Shantungosaurus*, was found in China. Duckbills with marvelous hollow head crests have mostly been found in North America.

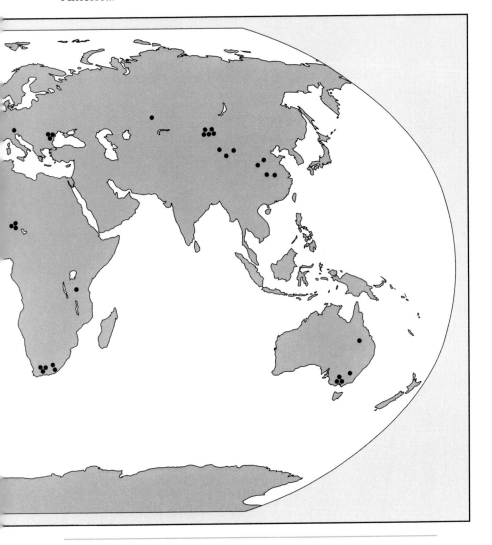

CHAPTER 4

ANATOMY

All organisms are made up of biological systems, such as the skeletal and muscular systems. The study of these structures is called anatomy. Studying the anatomy of an organism is different from studying how the structures are *used* by the organism. This type of study, physiology, is covered in the next chapter.

Dinosaurs Are Vertebrates

Dinosaurs are part of the lineage of animals known as vertebrates—animals with backbones. The first vertebrates were fish, followed by amphibians, reptiles, dinosaurs, and mammals and birds. To the best of our knowledge, the first vertebrates appeared about 520 million years ago in the form of jawless fish. Dinosaurs first walked the earth about 225 million years ago, nearly 300 million years after fish had begun to populate the oceans.

Regardless of whether they live in water, walk on land, or fly in air, all vertebrates share some common characteristics. The most basic common feature of the vertebrate body is that one side of the body is a mirror image of the other. This principle is called bilateral symmetry. A second common feature is that the organs of vertebrates have descended from what were basically the same organs in their ancestors. This idea is called the principle of homology.

Dinosaurs shared many similar skeletal features with other vertebrates, living and extinct. Even though we rarely, if ever, see the actual remains of soft tissue or organs of the dinosaurs—such as the brain, heart, lungs, liver, and gut—we can assume that they shared most of the internal organs of today's land-dwelling vertebrates. These ideas allow scientists to speculate about what a living dinosaur was really like.

The Dinosaur Hip

All dinosaurs are divided into two large groups based on the structure of their hipbones. The saurischian ("lizard-hipped") group is comprised of the two-legged carnivorous theropods; the four-legged, long-necked herbivorous sauropods; and the two-legged herbivorous prosauropods. The ornithischian ("bird-hipped") group includes all others, such as armored, horned, and duck-billed dinosaurs.

Both kinds of dinosaur hips allowed the hind legs to be attached underneath the body so that they could bear the entire weight of the creature. The hind legs were also connected to the hip with a ball-and-socket joint. This provided dinosaurs with increased flexibility and mobility over their reptile ancestors. The front legs were also positioned underneath the body to help bear the weight of those dinosaurs that walked on all fours.

The legs of a modern reptile, such as a crocodile or lizard, are attached at the sides of their body and do not support the full weight of their body while the creature is at rest. Reptiles lay their bellies on the ground and rise up only when they need to move. On the other hand, the position of a dinosaur was "always up." Dinosaurs must have been more active and energetic than today's reptiles simply because it required more stamina to hold up their body weight.

Dinosaur legs were designed more like those of mammals or birds but with some clear distinctions. While the joints in their shoulders and hips were flexible, those in the knees and elbows were not. This, combined with an ankle that was more like a door hinge than a ball and socket, restricted the

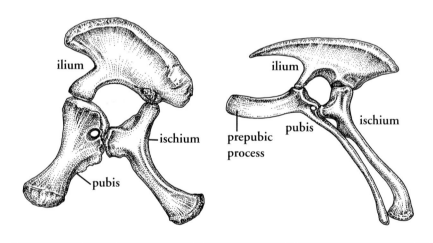

There are two kinds of dinosaur hips: saurischian ("lizard-hipped," left) and ornithiscian ("bird-hipped," right).

bending of a dinosaur's forelimbs and hind limbs in one plane of motion, forward and backward. Unlike humans and other mammals, which can move sideways with ease, a dinosaur had to turn its body if it wanted to move to the side. Dinosaurs would have made lousy soccer goalies.

The Ornithopod Body

Ornithopods evolved some of the most effective methods for eating plants ever seen. The duck-billed dinosaurs especially were equipped with astounding sets of teeth for continuously grinding tough vegetation. They had more teeth than any other known land animals. Ornithopods were mostly small creatures during the heyday of the large plant-chomping sauropods. But as the sauropods began to fade from the scene during the Early Cretaceous Period, ornithopods such as iguanodonts and duckbills grew larger and became the dominant plant eaters wherever they lived.

These plant eaters were some of the favorite prey of the theropods. Most ornithopods were probably slower runners than the meat eaters and survived mostly by breeding in large numbers. However, the skeletons of these creatures show that some ornithopods were not without defenses. *Iguanodon*, for example, had stout spikes for thumbs that could have been used to stab its attackers. Duck-billed dinosaurs might have used their hollow head crests to amplify their loud cries of warning when predators approached. The size and weight of the larger ornithopods were also enough to pose a danger to attackers. The stomp of a foot or the swing of a heavy tail could have easily crunched the bones of their adversaries.

The family tree of ornithopods includes creatures that varied widely in size. In addition to their bird-like hips, ornithopods had the following common characteristics:

- They walked on two legs (bipedal). The front legs of the ornithopods were shorter than their hind legs, indicating that they mostly walked on two legs. The front limbs of the larger ornithopods were stout enough to support their weight, however, so they sometimes leaned down to rest or walk on all fours. Smaller ornithopods such as *Hypsilophodon* were long-legged and fast runners. The larger ornithopods, including the iguanodonts and duckbills, had shorter hind legs than their meat-eating rivals, but they were still capable of running at a good pace when needed.

- They had three weight-supporting toes on their feet. The toes of the smaller ornithopods, such as *Heterodontosaurus* and *Hypsilophodon*, were sharp and pointed to help them run. The toes of larger ornithopods, such as *Iguanodon* and *Edmontosaurus*, were sturdy enough to hold the animal's heavy weight. These creatures all walked on their toes, rather than on their heels like bears and elephants.

- They had a long, stiffened tail that was held off the ground. This served as a counterbalance to the body when they were moving. The tails of some ornithopods, particularly the duck-billed dinosaurs, iguanodonts, and hypsilophodonts, had a matrix of bony rods joining individual back bones. These rods helped to stiffen and strengthen the tail so that it could be held out straight.

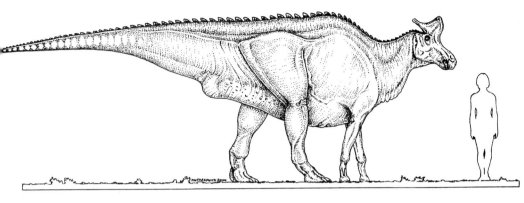

Ornithopod dinosaurs used their tails to help them balance. This *Lambeosaurus* is shown next to an adult for size comparison.

- The tip of the lower jaw was covered with a small bony beak. This beak was covered in life with horn. The beak was probably useful in snipping leaves and twigs.

- They had a flexible neck that was long and slender.

- Ornithopods had hands that were good for grasping, often with a thumblike finger. The hands of duckbills had less flexible fingers that were probably joined together with skin and looked like mittens. This can be seen in the remains of fossilized duckbill "mummies" that show how the hands and feet were thickly padded and wrapped in tough skin.

Dinosaur Skin

Dinosaur skin, like other soft body parts of these animals, was rarely if ever fossilized. The skin of dinosaurs easily decomposed and usually disappeared long before fossilization could take place. Although the skin itself would have decomposed, its pattern was sometimes preserved in the form of skin impressions.

Dinosaur skin impressions are the only clear evidence we have for what dinosaurs might have looked like on the outside. Artists who specialize in the reproduction of dinosaurs are particularly interested in skin impressions so that they can make their drawings accurate.

All of the evidence uncovered so far regarding dinosaur skin shows that they had nonoverlapping scales similar to those of the modern monitor lizard. These scales varied in size across different parts of the body. They were generally smaller,

Trace fossils of *Edmontosaurus* dinosaur skin show that they had scales similar to those of the modern monitor lizard. Many examples of duck-billed skin patterns have been discovered.

for flexibility, around the head and joints such as the neck and knees and larger along broad parts of the body and tail.

Fossilized skin impressions. A fossilized skin impression is not the dinosaur skin itself, but the pattern of the skin that was left in the mud where a dinosaur died. Skin impressions can often be associated with a specific kind of dinosaur if the fossilized bones are found nearby. Like trackways—the fossilized footprints of dinosaurs—skin impressions are known as trace fossils. They represent a trace of the dinosaur that made them, rather than being fossilized parts of the dinosaur itself. A number of good skin impressions have been found for herbivorous (plant-eating) dinosaurs, particularly the hadrosaurs.

Dinosaur mummies. There are some extremely rare conditions under which a dinosaur carcass may have been preserved with fossilized skin impressions intact. In these cases, the body of the dinosaur probably dried, undisturbed by scavengers, in the hot sun before being buried. The skin of the creature therefore became stretched tight over its bones. Even though the skin itself eventually disintegrated, the process of fossilization preserved its pattern throughout the specimen. The most famous dinosaur mummy is that of a duck-billed dinosaur on display at the American Museum of Natural History in New York City.

Skin color was never preserved in skin impressions or fossils. However, scientists can guess that the colors of dinosaurs varied, as color does in today's reptiles and birds. Some dinosaurs, especially smaller ones, may have had camouflaging colors to help them blend in with their surroundings. Color may have also been a way to tell the difference between males and females of the species, and therefore may have been a means for attracting a mate.

Ornithopod Skulls and Teeth

The different kinds of ornithopods differed widely in the design of the skull and jaws. They also varied in length from the tiny head of *Heterodontosaurus*—only 4.6 inches (11.7 centimeters) long—to the long and elaborately crested skull of *Parasaurolophus* ("similar crested lizard")—about 5 feet (1.5 meters) long.

All ornithopods were equipped with plant-eating teeth. The shape and arrangement of these teeth were very different from one kind of ornithopod to another. So, too, was the way in which they bit and munched vegetation. Most had a set of chewing teeth in the cheeks, and some had additional teeth in the front of the mouth for plucking and picking plant parts. Most of the vegetation that was available to these dinosaurs was tough and fibrous. It undoubtedly included twigs and other extremely coarse material that would have severely tested the chewing and digestive systems of these creatures. Over the course of their evolution, ornithopods became increasingly well adapted for eating these kinds of plants.

- *Heterodontosaurus*, one of the earliest ornithopods, had a set of chisel-shaped teeth along the sides of its mouth. Because the teeth were not tightly packed, the surfaces of the upper and lower teeth did not fit tightly together. Rather than grinding its food into a pulp

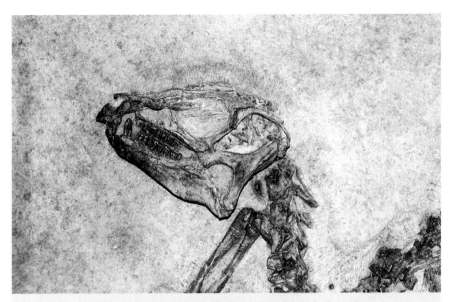

A *Heterodontosaurus* skull shows loosely-packed teeth.

before swallowing it, this dinosaur's teeth ripped the food into tiny shreds that the gut could easily digest. The lower jaw probably rotated as the mouth closed so that the dinosaur could rip plants between its upper and lower teeth. This dinosaur also had special teeth in the front of its mouth. These small incisors were used to pluck plant material from branches. A pair of small tusks, probably found only in the males, may have helped to grab its food.[1]

- *Hypsilophodon* ("high-crested tooth") and *Dryosaurus* ("oak lizard") had more advanced chewing teeth than *Heterodontosaurus*. Like their ancestor, they had chisel-shaped teeth, but the teeth were more tightly packed and overlapped when the jaw was closed to form a long cutting surface. They could grind and mince their food to a pulp before swallowing it, easing digestion. This was aided by a fleshy cheek pouch that could hold the food until it was well chewed. While *Hypsilophodon* still had some plucking teeth in the front of its jaw like *Heterodontosaurus*, these teeth were not present in *Dryosaurus* or most later ornithopods.

- With the evolution of *Iguanodon*, the set of grinding teeth found in related ornithopods advanced to become a sophisticated plant-chomping machine. The front of the jaws had become a tough, toothless beak for snipping off the twigs and other tough vegetation that this animal probably ate. The skull was long and narrow with an impressive row of ridged grinding teeth in each cheek. The upper and lower jaws each had about fifty chisel-shaped teeth. They were tightly packed to form a long grinding surface. Most animals that can grind food with their teeth, including cows and people, can move the lower jaw up and down as well as side to side. *Iguanodon* could not do this. Its lower jaw could only move up and down. However, it evolved a way to spread the upper jaw sideways to rub its teeth against the surface of the lower teeth. This movement was propelled by powerful jaw muscles, allowing *Iguanodon* to thoroughly grind the fibrous plants that it ate.[2]

- The hadrosaurs, or duck-billed dinosaurs, were further advanced in the efficiency of chewing. Like the iguanodonts, duckbills could move their upper jaws sideways to rub across the full surface of the lower teeth. Rather than the chisel-like teeth of other ornithopods, however, duck-billed dinosaurs developed tightly packed rows of interlocking teeth. The teeth were layered so that new teeth were continuously

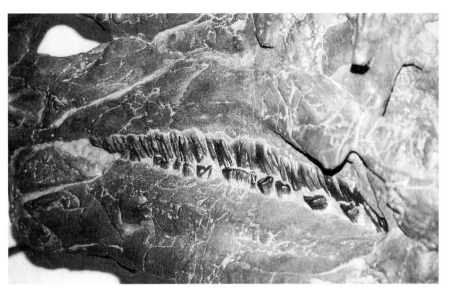

The teeth of ornithopods were made for grinding tough vegetation. *Iguanodon* (top) had up to one hundred chisel-shaped teeth that were more tightly packed than its predecessors, creating an improved chewing surface. The duck-billed dinosaur, *Kritosaurus* (bottom), had rows of interlocking teeth, forming a smooth surface for chewing and grinding its food.

Skulls of Different Ornithopods

Camptosaurus

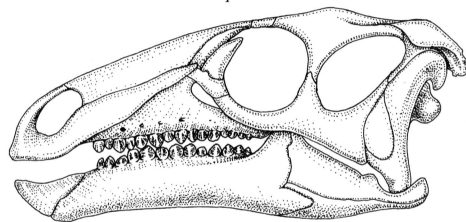

Hypsilophodon

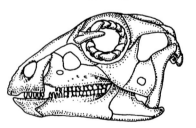

Heterodontosaurus

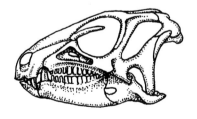

4 in (10 cm)

Dryosaurus

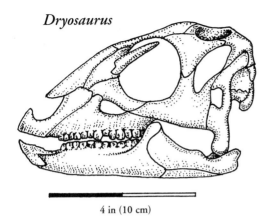

4 in (10 cm)

Corythosaurus

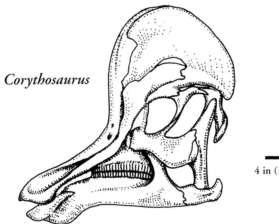

4 in (10 cm)

Iguanodon

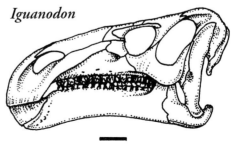

4 in (10 cm)

replacing old teeth. A duckbill's jaw had between 550 and 1400 such teeth, most lingering below the grinding surface. The teeth were so tightly packed that they formed a long, smooth pavement for chewing. These teeth were strong enough to pulverize the toughest plants with ease, yet adaptable to eat the softer flowering plants that were beginning to populate their world.

Helmets, Hatchets, and Hood Ornaments—Hadrosaurs on Parade

Hadrosaurs first appeared during the middle of the Late Cretaceous Period and were the last group of ornithopods to evolve. Their skeletons look so much alike that it is difficult to tell them apart without a skull. And when it comes to skulls, hadrosaurs had it all. In fact, the members of this family are divided into two groups based on the anatomy of the skull: Hadrosaurinae and Lambeosaurinae.

Hadrosaurinae had solid head crests or no head crest at all. They include the giants of the duck-billed dinosaurs, such as *Edmontosaurus* and *Shantungosaurus*. Their skulls were boxlike with a large nasal opening in the front. A few, such as *Saurolophus* ("crested lizard") and *Tsintaosaurus* ("Tsingtao lizard"), had a solid bony crest on the top of the head.

Lambeosaurinae had a long and narrow skull with a hollow crest on top. Different kinds of lambeosaurines had different crests.

What was the purpose of the hollow head crest? It was actually part of the nose. The nostrils were connected to the

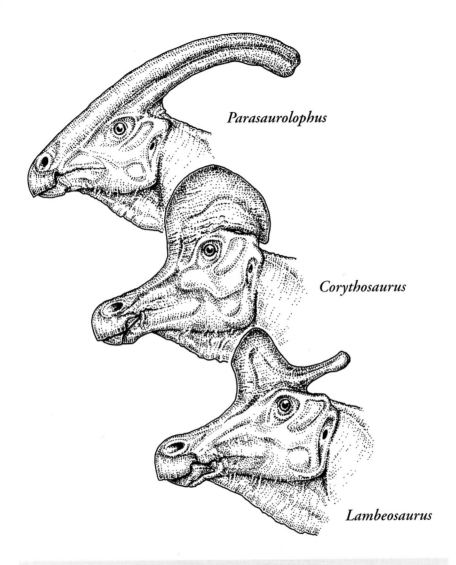

Parasaurolophus

Corythosaurus

Lambeosaurus

The head crests of duck-billed dinosaurs were actually giant extensions of their noses. Although they probably had several purposes, the most important were to help tell the difference between males and females and to create sounds.

throat by a hollow set of tubes, through which the dinosaur could breathe. But most other kinds of dinosaurs did not have such crests, so we must assume that hollow crests had a special function other than breathing. What other purpose could a crest have?

Crests came in a number of shapes. The crest of *Corythosaurus* ("helmet lizard") was rounded like a dinner plate standing on edge, its base being thick for air passages. One crest associated with *Lambeosaurus* resembles a hatchet. The long tubelike crest of *Parasaurolophus* was so long that it reached way behind the head and could touch the dinosaur's back.

Many ideas have been suggested over the years for the purpose of the head crest. One early theory about the long looping crest of *Parasaurolophus* was that it may have been used like a snorkel. But since there is no evidence that these crests had a breathing hole at the end, this idea is no longer accepted.

These crests probably served more than one purpose. It is likely that these supersized noses improved the dinosaur's sense of smell. A relatively defenseless creature such as a hadrosaur could use a powerful sense of smell to pick up the scent of its enemies.

The crest probably helped members of the same species recognize one another. This would have been important to further the species. Peter Dodson did a study of hadrosaur head crests and determined that they first became prominent when the animals reached the age of sexual maturity.

Furthermore, females probably had crests shaped differently than males. The smaller-crested members of the species were probably the females.[3] Being able to tell the boys from the girls would have made the dinosaurs' job of finding a mate easier. The shape and color of the crest may have made one male or female more attractive than another. It would have also indicated the relative age and sexual maturity of each sex. In the world of animal matchmaking, these kinds of visual clues are important for bringing together healthy mates. Healthy, strong mates are more likely to produce babies that will live long and further the species.

Another function of the crest might have been to vocalize sounds. The dinosaur could blow air through the tubes and hollow chambers of the crest to create bellowing sounds, not unlike that of an antique car horn or elephant. These sounds may have been important to hadrosaur communication. They could have used their voices to warn of approaching danger, to call for help, or to express themselves in other instances.

Another idea about the purpose of the head crest came from a recent study of *Parasaurolophus.* It was once believed that the long crest of this dinosaur contained two hollow tubes running alongside each other, one for each nostril. The examination of a new and more complete specimen of the crest revealed that the two tubes from the nostrils actually branched out into as many as six tubes, and that there are air chambers in various parts of the crest. Not only would this have allowed the creature to make a richer variety of sounds, but the crest may have also helped regulate the temperature of the dinosaur.

Lambeosaurus

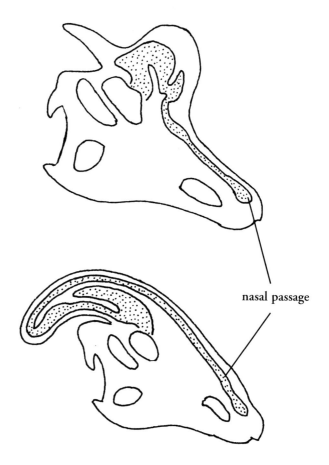

nasal passage

Parasaurolophus

Hadrosaur head crests were extensions of the nasal passages. These dinosaurs could probably create a wide range of distinctive sounds by blowing air through them.

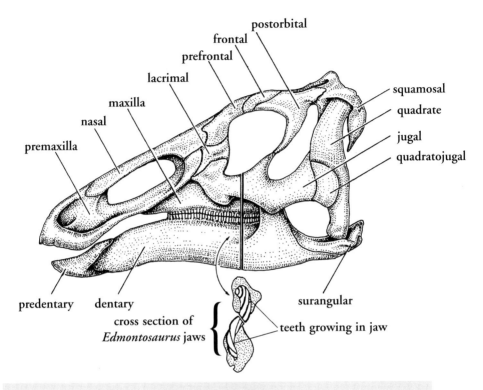

Edmontosaurus skull

The inside of the *Parasaurolophus* crest was lined with blood vessels. Heat could have been gathered by the crest if the head was turned toward the sun or released when held in the shadows. The air passages in the crest would have allowed it to transfer heat more efficiently.[4]

Anatomy of the *Edmontosaurus* Skull. Skulls are composed of many small parts. Each part has its own name. Most of these parts are found in all ornithopod skulls, but they vary in size and shape depending on the particular kind of dinosaur. Dinosaur skulls are often found in fragments, so paleontologists must be able to recognize dinosaur types from the smallest of pieces. The elements found in the ornithopod skull are illustrated on the previous page using *Edmontosaurus.*

CHAPTER 5

PHYSIOLOGY

The skeletal anatomy of a dinosaur tells only part of the picture of these once-living creatures. To imagine what they were like in life, scientists have to consider how the structures in their bodies worked together and were adapted to their environment and lifestyles. The study of these structures and functions is called physiology.

The physiology of ornithopods is understood by comparing the evidence from fossils to the anatomy and physiology of today's creatures. Other physical evidence, such as trackways, has also been used to piece together what we know about the ornithopods and other dinosaurs.

Brains and Smarts

How smart were dinosaurs? This question is not easy to answer. After all, what *is* intelligence? Intelligence can be described as the ability to process information, or to learn. Since this is something we will never be able to observe in dinosaurs, we must rely on other clues to intelligence that are found in the fossil record. Chief among these is the size of a dinosaur's brain in comparison to the size of its body.

In examining many kinds of living animals, scientists have found a relationship between intelligence and the size of the brain compared to the size of the creature's body. A species whose brain is large for its body size is usually more intelligent. This evidence allows scientists to compare the intelligence of animals of different body sizes, say a Pekingese dog with an Irish wolfhound. By this measure, mammals and birds are considered to be more intelligent than fish, amphibians, and reptiles. What makes humans so unusual is that our brain size is seven times greater than should be expected for a creature with our body size.

The brain, like most other soft tissues and organs, has not been preserved in the fossil record. However, the approximate size of a dinosaur's brain can be determined by measuring and casting the cavity in the skull where the brain once was. This cavity is called the braincase. Unfortunately, most dinosaur skull material is incomplete and does not include the braincase. Even when the braincase is present, the space is not often well preserved due to the compression and crushing of the skull during fossilization. Measurements have thus far been made for less than 5 percent of all known dinosaurs, so much work remains in this area.[1] Luckily, several good examples of fossil braincases exist for ornithopod dinosaurs.

How smart were ornithopods? Based on brain-to-body ratios, predatory dinosaurs may have been the Albert Einsteins of the dinosaur kingdom, but ornithopods were no dummies.

Their potential brain power was second only to that of the theropods in the world of the dinosaurs. In some cases, ornithopods shared a high brain weight-to-body weight ratio with many of their meat-eating rivals. This made them somewhat brighter than other kinds of dinosaurs, perhaps even comparable to some modern mammals. Many other dinosaurs, though not as gifted, were still comparable to modern crocodilians and reptiles when it came to the size of their brain compared to body weight.[2]

Senses

Herbivorous creatures rely on their senses to locate food and avoid danger. A good sense of smell might pick up the scent of a grove of tasty vegetation or a stalking predator over the next hill. A good sense of hearing, like smell, provides clues to the presence of carnivores before they can be seen. Keen eyesight is important for finding food and noticing the movements of an approaching meat eater.

The senses of hearing, smell, and vision were certainly important to the ornithopods. Evidence for these senses can be seen by studying the braincase and other parts of a dinosaur's skull.

Holes in the Head. The braincase in a dinosaur skull holds clues to the many connections between the brain and other parts of the body. Evidence of these nerve connections can be seen in the form of holes in the braincase through which nerves were once threaded to attach the brain to other organs.

The brains of modern vertebrates—particularly reptiles and birds—are similar in many ways. The sense of smell is located at the front of the brain in the olfactory lobe, and vision is concentrated in an optic lobe near the center. Observing the kinds of nerve connections that exist in today's animals can help a paleontologist identify the locations of similar features in dinosaur skulls.

Vision. Evidence for the size of the eyes comes from the size of the eye sockets in the skull, as well as the occasional preservation of thin bony eye rings—sclerotic rings—that encircled the outer edge, or equator, of the eyeball. Eye rings are seen today in birds and some modern reptiles. Sclerotic rings held the shape of the eyeball and may have helped the eye focus for sharp eyesight.[3]

The eye socket in most ornithopods was quite large. There is also evidence for sclerotic rings in several ornithopods, including hypsilophodonts and hadrosaurs.[4] These sometimes measure between 2.5 and 3 inches (6.4 and 7.6 centimeters) in diameter, a truly big eye. Large eye sockets and sclerotic rings indicate that ornithopods probably had excellent eyesight.

Smell. In those cases where a braincase has been preserved—such as the skull of *Iguanodon*—the olfactory lobe in the front of the brain is large. This suggests that smell was keen in these dinosaurs and other ornithopods as well. The ability to smell the scent of an approaching predator could have meant the difference between life and death for animals that were otherwise somewhat defenseless. This would have given them time to regroup their herd into a tighter, safer formation or to run for safety.

Hearing. The hearing power of dinosaurs is not clearly understood. We know that dinosaur skulls include a hollowed-out cavity behind the eyes where the hearing mechanism once resonated, but just how acute it was is difficult to guess. Paleontologists have been fortunate, however, in the study of ornithopod hearing. Several specimens of hadrosaurs include a delicate hearing bone in the back of the skull. One excellent *Iguanodon* skull includes the fossilized inner ear cavity, including those areas used for hearing and balance.[5] These clues are among the best evidence ever for the hearing power of dinosaurs. They tell us that ornithopods had acute hearing.

Growth Rate

Newly hatched dinosaurs were small, yet they sometimes grew to enormous sizes that were anywhere from ten times to thousands of times their original weight. What can the fossil record tell us about how fast the dinosaurs grew from hatchling to adult?

To understand how fast dinosaurs grew, scientists need three things. The first is a keen knowledge of how fast modern reptiles, birds, and other animals grow. Then they can keep their guesses about dinosaurs in perspective. Information about reptile growth is abundant. Also, reptiles continue to grow throughout their lives, unlike birds and mammals, which reach a peak size soon after reaching sexual maturity. Scientists would like to find out which of these growth patterns applied to dinosaurs.

The second thing needed to understand the growth rates of dinosaurs is a series of fossil skeletons for a given kind of dinosaur that represents several life stages. This is available in abundance for some hadrosaurs, especially *Maiasaura* ("good-mother lizard").

The third thing needed to understand how fast a dinosaur grew is a way in which to connect what is seen in the bones to the growth span of a dinosaur. One attempt to do this uses microscopic studies of dinosaur bone. A magnified cross section of bone can reveal clues about dinosaur growth.

At one extreme, some bones formed in a smooth, continuous pattern. This indicates that the dinosaur was growing continuously and rapidly. At the other extreme, some bone tissue formed in curious rings called lines of arrested growth. These growth rings are much like the seasonal rings in cross sections of tree trunks. This phenomenon is also seen in the bones of modern reptiles. It represents an annual period when growth slows down, perhaps during a cool season when the animal is less active for an extended period.

Some dinosaurs have both kinds of bone tissue. This means that they grew at different rates at different times in their lives. It appears that they grew rapidly until they reached adult size, then they slowed down but still continued growing.

There is an abundance of evidence for several ornithopods that they grew rapidly for several years before slowing down when they reached adulthood. What is most surprising is just

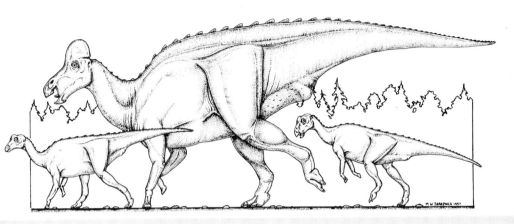

How fast did ornithopods grow? Scientists are still studying this question. Scientists believe *Hypacrosaurus*, shown here with two juveniles, grew rapidly at a young age, until they reached near adult size.

how fast they grew. *Maiasaura* from Montana required only about seven years to reach its maximum size of 30 feet (9 meters).[6] It reached adult size about twice as fast as crocodiles and humans.[7] During its first few years of growth, it did not show evidence of growth rings, suggesting that it grew continuously without seasonal interruptions.[8] Growing up fast would have been important because these dinosaurs were defenseless against predators until they were large enough to use their size for protection.

Studies of other ornithopods, including the dryosaur *Dryosaurus*,[9] the hypsilophodont *Orodromeus* ("mountain runner"),[10] and the hadrosaur *Hypacrosaurus* ("very high ridged lizard"),[11] all show moderate to rapid growth at a young age and an absence of growth rings until these dinosaurs reached near adult size.

While microscopic bone studies provide some truly intriguing information about possible dinosaur growth rates, they also lead to additional questions. Counting growth rings in bones like those in a tree are not as reliable as originally thought. Different bones in the same dinosaur skeleton may have different numbers of growth rings.

Aside from how fast the ornithopods grew, can paleontologists tell how long an individual may have lived? This question is also tricky. Evidence from growth rings in the bone cannot answer this question, because a dinosaur could have lived many more years after its bones stopped producing growth rings. A scientist would also need to know more about a dinosaur's metabolism. Best guesses for the life span of a dinosaur come from observing modern-day animals and making some assumptions about size and metabolism. It is possible that small ornithopods lived between fifteen and twenty years and that larger species lived for more than fifty.

Were Dinosaurs Warm-Blooded?

Scientists think that dinosaurs were not the slow and sluggish creatures that they once thought them to be. Dinosaurs were built for action and could probably have moved quite fast when needed. Some dinosaurs also grew rapidly, outpacing the growth rate often seen in modern mammals. But not all dinosaurs were alike in this way. Some grew quite slowly, and there were many others in between.

Does this tell us whether dinosaurs were endotherms (warm-blooded) or ectotherms (cold-blooded)? This is a

Fruitachampsa, a form of crocodilian from the Jurassic Period of Colorado, may have raided the nests of the ornithopod *Dryosaurus altus*.

question that many paleontologists have argued. Unfortunately, there is no simple answer or single piece of fossil evidence that can tell us for sure.

There are two factors that determine whether an animal is warm- or cold-blooded. One is the source of heat. Was it internal, as in endotherms, or external, as in ectotherms? The other factor is the consistency of body temperature. Was it constant or variable?

If we look at today's animals, we can see that small and large mammals are warm-blooded and that reptiles of all sizes are cold-blooded. Dinosaurs were clearly evolved from reptiles, so they were originally thought to be cold-blooded.

However, current thinking shows dinosaurs were highly active and unique kinds of creatures, clearly different from other reptiles in many ways. How could they be so active *and* be cold-blooded?

The answer lies in the huge size of dinosaurs. There are no creatures quite like them alive today. But there is evidence that being cold-blooded does not rule out that a creature can be active and energetic and maintain a constant body temperature. Instead of obtaining most of its body heat from its own internal metabolism, as with warm-blooded creatures, a cold-blooded animal may use a method called gigantothermy to maintain its temperature.

Gigantothermy relies on a combination of biologic and environmental factors to work:[12]

A warm, temperate, or subtropical climate, such as that enjoyed by the dinosaurs. Heat absorbed during the day would be retained for many hours past dark in a large dinosaur.[13]

Large body size. The larger the body, the more likely that it would retain heat that was absorbed from the environment or produced internally through normal metabolic processes. The greater the volume, the greater the heat retention.

Layers of body insulation. Layers of fat were probably capable of retaining body heat.

A digestive process producing heat. Food is digested using a gastric fermentation process that produces heat as a by-product. The mere volume of the gut of dinosaurs suggests that a lot of heat was generated this way.

Special adaptations of the circulatory system. Blood flow and the circulatory path is used to pass heat from the core or gut of the dinosaur to its surface, where it can be safely shed to avoid overheating. The extensive surface area of the body, including the long tails, may have been part of the strategy for shedding excess heat.

All of the above reasons made it possible for ornithopods and other forms of large dinosaurs to maintain high body temperatures while still having lower cold-blooded metabolic rates. This could have made a significant difference in the survival of the ornithopods, because a lower metabolism required them to eat less than if they had been warm-blooded. Lower food requirements would have allowed a larger population to be supported than if metabolic rates and food requirements were higher.

But the theory of gigantothermy comes with a significant problem. It does not account for the metabolic process of small dinosaurs or a dinosaur while it was young and growing, before it reached a size at which gigantothermy could take over. This remains one of the puzzles of dinosaur metabolism. Perhaps the warm environment was enough to keep them active. This, plus the fact that they were eating more as they grew, might account for their maintaining a constant body temperature without the benefit of gigantothermy.

Ornithopod Speed

How fast could ornithopods run? You may think there could be no answer. After all, no one has been able to set a dinosaur loose on a racetrack and time it with a stopwatch. But there are ways that paleontologists have tried to answer this question.

Fossil footprints, or trackways, left by dinosaurs are the best clues to the speed of dinosaurs. It is not always easy to identify the maker of the tracks. Hypsilophodonts and tenontosaurs had claws very similar to those of theropods, so it is easy to misinterpret these tracks.

Some of the most commonly found dinosaur footprints are those of iguanodonts and hadrosaurs. They are large and show the impressions of padded feet and three blunt toes. The identity of the track makers is generally based on the time period in which they were made and the kinds of ornithopod fossils found in the same area. Ornithopod tracks of this kind from the Early Cretaceous Period are most usually those of iguanodonts, and those from the Late Cretaceous belong to hadrosaurs.

Some ornithopod trackways are extensive and stretch for many miles. They sometimes show the walking pattern of a large herd.[14]

Having the trackways is not enough, however. A stopwatch is not going to do any good, either. To understand dinosaur speed from trackways, scientists use the length of the strides, the leg length of the dinosaur from the ground to the hip, and a mathematical formula to calculate the speed. A scientist named Robert McNeill Alexander worked out a formula to calculate speed from trackways that is widely used today.[15]

Alexander applied his formula to several kinds of theropod

trackways. The top theropod speed he calculated from the trackways of a small theropod, probably of the ostrich-dinosaur variety, was 27 miles per hour (44 kilometers per hour). This is faster than a human can run, somewhat slower than a racehorse, and about the same as a galloping antelope.[16]

Many ornithopod trackways have been discovered and studied. In contrast to the faster theropods, hadrosaurs, iguanodonts, and other larger ornithopods mostly moved at a slow walk of about 1.6 to 5 miles per hour (2.6 to 8 kilometers per hour).[17] Some trackways indicate that they had a running speed of between 10 and 14 miles per hour (17 and 22.5 kilometers per hour).[18] Though these speeds were not fast enough to outdistance most meat-eating dinosaurs, they show that ornithopods were not always as slow-moving as was once thought.

Males and Females

Telling the males from the females is not easy from skeletons. Paleontologists can be comfortable about doing this only when an abundance of skeletons from the same kind of dinosaur can be compared. They look for differences that could distinguish the males from the females. These traits are the result of sexual dimorphism—naturally occurring differences between the sexes of the same kind of animal. These come in the form of size, shape, and behavioral differences.[19] In nature, these differences help identify the males from the females and may also have other important functions. For example, male elephants have tusks that are used during combat or jousting with other males. Male deer use antlers to lock and wrestle with rivals to win the favor of a female.

Sexual dimorphism has been observed in three kinds of ornithopods. One of the earliest ornithopods, *Heterodontosaurus*, is usually found with a pair of canine tusks. Another specimen has been found that has an identical skull except that it lacks the tusks. It has been suggested that the tusks were found only in the males, although the tuskless variety may also have been a juvenile whose tusks had not yet formed.[20]

The ornithopod *Hypsilophodon* shows a variation in the spine that may signal a difference between males and females. All dinosaurs have several fused, or joined, back bones that are

Specimens of *Heterodontosaurus* have been found with and without tusks. Perhaps the tusks were only found in the males, or the tuskless variety was a juvenile whose tusks had not yet formed.

connected to the hip. The number of these fused back bones does not usually vary for a given kind of dinosaur. However, in *Hypsilophodon* specimens, it has been noticed that the number of fused back bones may be either five or six. It has been suggested that this is the result of sexual dimorphism.[21]

In the world of hadrosaurs, scientists have discovered an abundance of interesting skulls that help distinguish one kind from another. It also turns out that these skulls provide clues as to which were the males and which were the females. But this was not always understood.

Until 1975, there were many more individual species of crested hadrosaurs on the books than there are today. This is because of the pioneering work of paleontologist Peter Dodson, who reexamined the world of crested duck-billed dinosaurs. Until his work, new duckbill specimens were often named based largely on variations in the shape of the head crest. Dodson showed that many of these crested dinosaurs— once believed to be different species—were merely males or females of already classified dinosaurs.[22] The hollow head crests of several species came in two distinct shapes. Those individuals with the larger of the two forms are thought to be the males. *Corythosaurus*, *Lambeosaurus*, and *Parasaurolophus* are all examples of duck-billed dinosaurs whose skulls show two distinctly different crest shapes as a result of sexual dimorphism.

CHAPTER 6

EGGS AND BABIES

Dinosaurs, like their bird descendants and most known reptiles, hatched from eggs. More than 220 dinosaur egg sites have been discovered, and three quarters of these are from North America and Asia.[1] Most that have been found date from the Late Cretaceous Period.

Our knowledge of the lifestyle and behavior of ornithopod dinosaurs has been greatly enriched by the discovery of their fossilized eggs, nests, and young. No other kind of dinosaur has left us more evidence about how they lived and behaved. The discoveries are due mostly to the pioneering work of pale-ontologist John "Jack" Horner. Together with his students and coworkers from Montana State University, Horner has spent many years studying the stunning remains of eggs, nests, and skeletons found at numerous fossil sites in northwestern Montana.

We know from these discoveries that at least some kinds of ornithopods nested in colonies and took care of their young until they were able to leave the nest on their own. Many of these eggs and nests belonged to *Maiasaura*, or "good-mother lizard," so named because of evidence that these duck-billed dinosaurs cared for their young. Their behavior is strikingly similar to that of modern birds.

From 1978 to 1983, Horner and his colleagues unearthed a treasure trove of *Maiasaura* eggs and babies. Dating from about 80 million years ago—in the Late Cretaceous Period— were three nesting sites consisting of 14 nests, 42 eggs, and 31 babies.[2] Larger specimens of *Maiasaura* at various stages of growth were also found, although a good adult skeleton is still lacking. The discoveries were astounding in many ways. In only a few short years, Horner's team not only uncovered a new species of hadrosaur, but also succeeded in painting a colorful and astonishingly complete picture of its lifestyle, growth stages, behavior, and ecosystem. It was perhaps the most revealing dinosaur discovery of the entire twentieth century.

The discovery of *Maiasaura*, its nests, and babies began with a trip to a rock shop in a tiny Montana town in 1978. It was there that Jack Horner and his friend Robert Makela were given a coffee can full of baby dinosaur bones. Marion Brandvold, the owner of the shop, later took the two paleon-tologists to the field site where the bones had been found, and the hunt for baby dinosaurs was under way. This first dig resulted in the discovery of a *Maiasaura* nest with the remains of fifteen 3-foot- (1-meter-) long duck-billed dinosaurs still inside. The work of a few days expanded steadily over the course of a few years as the team continued to discover nests, eggs, and the remains of maiasaurs of different sizes.

The eggs were laid in bowl-shaped nests about 6.5 feet

Maiasaura babies may have remained in the nest for an extended period, perhaps as long as eight or nine months. During this time, a parent dinosaur would have brought food to them.

(2 meters) across and 2.5 feet (75 centimeters) deep. The mother *Maiasaura* may have dug out the nest in the mud with her hind feet and shaped it into a mound with her hands and muzzle. The hollowed-out mound of mud was then covered with vegetation such as pine needles to protect and incubate the eggs.[3] There were up to twenty eggs per nest.[4] Most puzzling was the fact that the eggs were always found in tiny fragments and with no obvious pattern to their arrangement. It was as if they had been trampled underfoot repeatedly for a long time. It became obvious that this is exactly what had happened when the scientists took a close look at the bones of the babies that were found in the nest.

The baby *Maiasaura* dinosaurs found in the nests were sometimes up to 3 feet (1 meter) long. There were two intriguing features of the skeletons that have been interpreted in different ways. The teeth of the young were well worn and the joints in their legs were weak, which would have made it difficult for them to move about. Horner thinks this means the hatchlings were eating but not capable of leaving the nest to fend for themselves. It became apparent to Horner that the *Maiasaura* babies remained in the nest for an extended period, perhaps as long as eight or nine months.[5] If this were the case, then the young dinosaurs were defenseless and helpless while they were living in the nest. This could mean only one thing: There was an adult dinosaur looking over them, protecting them from predators and bringing food to the nest for them to eat, like birds caring for their young. The reason the eggshells had been pulverized in the nests was that they had been stomped on for many months by a brood of active, nest-bound youngsters. Horner's view of the evidence, and a picture forming of a large adult hadrosaur taking care of its nestlings, inspired him to name the dinosaur *Maiasaura*, meaning "good-mother lizard."

Horner's interpretation of the *Maiasaura* evidence was not accepted by all. Because no *Maiasaura* embryo has yet been found inside an intact fossil egg, it is possible that Horner's "hatchlings" may actually be unhatched embryos. This would explain their extremely small size and undeveloped leg joints. Even the evidence of worn teeth in Horner's *Maiasaura* hatchlings does not prove with certainty that the specimens were not embryos. Horner himself discovered the embryonic remains of another ornithopod, *Hypacrosaurus*, that showed tooth wear prior to being hatched.[6]

Making Horner's portrait of hadrosaur family life even more fascinating was the fact that the nests themselves were part of a larger nesting ground. Each nest was about 23 feet (7 meters) apart, which is about equal to the estimated average length of an adult *Maiasaura.*[7] This suggests that the dinosaurs nested together, in peace, and made room for an entire herd in a manner similar to bird colonies today. Nesting in colonies would have made good sense for these dinosaurs. Because the young were helpless for many months, keeping them together in a nest would have protected them from predators and given them time to grow so that they could blend in with the herd. Except for an occasional raid by a small theropod such as *Troodon,* a nesting ground with hundreds of nests and adult *Maiasaura* would have made its own safe haven for the duck-billed dinosaurs living within its bounds.

Horner's team also found several deposits of nests and eggs in different layers of rock. This strongly suggests that the dinosaurs returned to the same spot to lay their eggs. This led Horner to picture a large herd of migrating *Maiasaura,* perhaps 10,000 strong,[8] making their way back to the same nesting grounds year after year.[9]

The fate that doomed this nesting ground and its many inhabitants must have been swift and fierce. It was a fairly flat plain 80 million years ago, laced with streams and an inland sea about a hundred miles away. The area probably flooded seasonally with the coming of torrential rains. Each year, after the breeding season was over, some of the leftover nests were probably covered with mud during the rainy season. But it was not a flood or rain that sealed the fate of Horner's herd of nesting duckbills. They appear to have died from a massive volcanic eruption that rained hot ash and poisonous gases down on them. There they were laid to rest, covered with the smoky dust of volcanic cinder, entombed in the earth, doomed to become fossils that would reveal their most amazing story only millions of years later.

CHAPTER 7

FEEDING HABITS AND ADAPTATIONS

Ornithopods, especially the iguanodonts and hadrosaurs, were some of the most impressive chewers ever to walk the earth. They went about the business of eating with a highly advanced set of choppers that has never been equaled. This is only somewhat impressive when compared to mammals, many of which have excellent jaw adaptations for grazing on vegetation. But what these dinosaurs achieved was truly astounding when compared to other reptiles and many other plant-eating dinosaurs, most of which did not have chewing teeth. Ornithopods—along with the horned dinosaurs—were marvelous chewing machines.[1]

What Did They Eat?

As browsers, ornithopods ate vegetation that covered the ground or that was low hanging, such as bushes and the lower branches of trees. They probably leaned over, resting their weight on their front limbs while slowly making their way through a buffet of leaves. The larger members of a herd could rise up and reach as high as 12 or 13 feet (about 4 meters) above the ground.[2]

Plant life on Earth changed dramatically during the 135-million-year rise and evolution of the ornithopods. Three major kinds of land plants were common during the different periods of ornithopod development, providing the following possible dinner menu: [3]

Pteridophytes. Pteridophytes included the ferns, horse-tails, and club mosses. Ferns came in forms that hugged the ground but also as trees with an unadorned stemlike trunk with a single growing point at the top. These plants generally required a moist environment, but they were fast-growing and could be grazed without killing the plant, making them an excellent renewable source of food. These plants were available throughout the history of the ornithopods. They were an especially important source of food for the earliest ornithopods, including the heterodontosaurs and hypsilophodonts.

Gymnosperms. Gymnosperms were two groups of primitive seed plants, the conifers and the cycads. They reproduced by means of a naked seed, in contrast to the angiosperms, which had a seed enclosed within a fruit. Today's conifers, including pine trees and other evergreens, existed in the form of small shrubs and large trees. Another branch of the conifer group included the cypress and bald cypress families and broad-leaved ginkgo trees. The cycads were mostly short plants with bulbous or palmlike trunks. They were capped with fronds reminiscent of those on palm trees.

Gymnosperms were not moist or soft. They were not an easy food to digest, nor did they contain abundant nutrients. They were gradually displaced as a source of food by the rise of the flowering plants, or angiosperms, in the late part of the Cretaceous Period.

Angiosperms. Angiosperms are flowering plants, the last of the major plant groups to evolve. They were distinguished by having a seed borne within a fruit, unlike the gymnosperms, which bore naked seeds. They first appeared in the middle Cretaceous Period. They diversified and spread rapidly in the form of flowering shrubs to become the dominant plant group by the end of the Cretaceous.[4] They reproduced and grew more quickly than gymnosperms, making them abundantly available as dinosaur food. The foliage of angiosperms was generally more digestible, moist, and nutritionally sound than either pteridophytes or gymnosperms. The ability of these plants to spread and grow quickly made them ideally suited for the veggie-munching machinery of the latter ornithopods.

If the sauropods were nature's most effective plant-eating creatures during the Jurassic and Early Cretaceous Periods, then iguanodonts and hadrosaurs were the champs of the middle and later Cretaceous. There is reason to believe that they displaced sauropods as the planet's dominant plant eaters because they were better adapted for browsing and chewing the angiosperms. The fossil record indicates that the

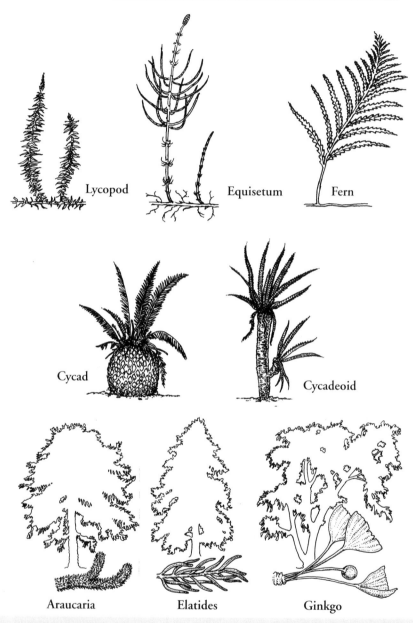

Lycopod

Equisetum

Fern

Cycad

Cycadeoid

Araucaria

Elatides

Ginkgo

Plants that the ornithopods ate throughout their reign included the pterido-phytes, gymnosperms, and angiosperms.

sauropods disappeared from the Northern Hemisphere as the angiosperms rose. At the same time, as if to fill a plant-eating gap in the ecology of the planet, the iguanodonts and hadrosaurs rose to dominate the world of herbivorous animals.

Grasses, a staple in the diet of today's plant eaters, did not appear until after the demise of the dinosaurs.

Adaptations for Feeding

The posture and height of ornithopods gave them access to both ground cover and higher plants. While the long-necked and taller sauropods commanded the treetops, the iguanodonts and duck-billed dinosaurs ruled an area from ground level to about 12 to 13 feet (about 4 meters) high. Being able to stand on two or four legs extended their eating range beyond that of the strictly four-legged herbivores such as the armored and horned dinosaurs. Ornithopods had flexible necks for reaching into and around the plants they were eating. All had hands that could grasp the trunks and limbs of trees and shrubs. This allowed them to hold a plant still while they stripped it of leaves and twigs with their beaks and teeth.

Hard evidence for what the ornithopods ate has been found with some fossil specimens. The famous duck-billed dinosaur mummy mentioned earlier (see page 43) contained what may have been the fossilized remains of the hadrosaur's last meal. It consisted of pine needles, bark fragments, pieces of pine cones, and berries.[5] Scientists cannot be certain, however, that these plant parts were actually inside the gut of the dinosaur when it died or washed into the carcass later from the surrounding soil. In either case, these needles and cones are from plants that grow in a dry environment, further proof that duck-billed dinosaurs did not live mostly in swamps or watery environments as had first been presumed after their discovery in the nineteenth century.

Additional evidence of a dinosaur's meal may come in the form of fossilized dinosaur dung, or coprolites. While it is difficult to know for sure which kind of dinosaur produced a given coprolite, the evidence sometimes points to a likely candidate. Such is the case for a group of large, blocky coprolites from the Late Cretaceous sediments of Montana. This fossil

The posture and height of ornithopods gave them access to both ground cover and higher plants.

dung is composed primarily of woody conifer stem fragments that must have been chewed quite vigorously. The coprolites are found in close proximity to the skeletal remains of the duck-billed dinosaur *Maiasaura,* the most likely producer of these coprolites.[6]

The evolution of ornithopod jaws and teeth was discussed earlier in this book. How they digested their food is also of interest. From the mouth, the chewed-up vegetation passed into the gut of the animal, where it was fermented and digested to extract nutrients. The stomach must have been adapted to squeeze every possible ounce of nutrition from the tough, woody, food sources that made up much of an ornithopod's diet. It is likely that, like an elephant, an ornithopod only fully digested about 40 or 50 percent of what it ate, the rest being too tough to process.[7] Only the duck-billed dinosaurs, the last of the ornithopods, may have had an easier time digesting their food because their diet consisted largely of the softer, nutrient-rich flowering plants.

CHAPTER 8

ORNITHOPOD DEFENSES

Ornithopod dinosaurs lacked the obvious defenses of the armored, horned, and club-bearing plant eaters. They were most certainly one of the favorite entrées on any predator's dinner menu. Yet they survived in populations that were apparently still growing at the end of the age of dinosaurs.

Although an occasional tyrannosaur was certainly a cause for concern, ornithopods were probably bothered more frequently by smaller predators such as *Deinonychus* ("terrible claw"), *Velociraptor* ("swift robber") and *Troodon* ("wounding tooth"). These swift-moving meat eaters could do their damage by darting in and out of a herd or nesting ground to snatch the young and defenseless with their hands or teeth. Some may have also ganged up on larger members of an ornithopod herd that had been cut off from their group. There is strong evidence that *Deinonychus* hunted in packs and that one of its favorite targets was *Tenontosaurus* ("tendon lizard," after the stiff tendons in its tail). The remains of this medium-sized ornithopod were first discovered in Montana along with several specimens of *Deinonychus.*

The success of the ornithopods was due mostly to their adaptation to the environment. Their complicated jaws and teeth were ideally suited for chewing the extremely tough vegetation they often ate. Their bodies were bulky, yet flexible and mobile, allowing them to move with ease and probably at surprising speeds when necessary. Their social behavior, as suggested from the study of *Maiasaura,* also contributed to the ability of ornithopods to fend off adversity and beat the odds for survival. But when faced with predatory dinosaurs large and small, how did ornithopods defend themselves? Their methods seem to have been simple and undramatic.

Speed. Small- to medium-sized ornithopods, such as *Heterodontosaurus, Hypsilophodon,* and *Tenontosaurus,* were swift creatures. They were built for running and agility, with long legs, slender bodies, and stiffened tails that improved their balance. Shifting the tail back and forth would have allowed a dinosaur to change directions quickly, a tactic that the smaller ornithopods probably used to evade pursuers.[1] They probably depended on speed to escape the predators of their time, including *Coelophysis* ("hollow form"), *Allosaurus* ("different lizard"), *Deinonychus,* and other small dromaeosaurs. Iguanodonts and hadrosaurs were huge compared to their tiny ancestors. Although running for their lives was probably not their primary means of defense, they were certainly

Dryosaurus, pursued by a meat-eating *Allosaurus*, was a 12-foot dinosaur with no teeth at the front of its jaws.

capable of moving quickly when necessary, especially for short distances.

Size. The iguanodonts and hadrosaurs had the advantage of size and bulk over many predators of the time. The average length of an adult hadrosaur was 30 feet (9 meters), and a few giants reached 49 feet (15 meters) in length. They were certainly vulnerable as youngsters, but once they grew to adult size, they were too large and risky a target for even the largest predators. Predatory dinosaurs were built for power and speed but were leaner than the large ornithopods. The desperate motions of an iguanodont or duck-billed dinosaur under attack would pose serious risks to a predator. The force of an iguanodont stomp, the shove of a four-ton duckbill, or the bone-crunching fall of an ornithopod on top of a carnivore could bring a swift end to any such Mesozoic wrestling match.

Defensive weapons. Ornithopods were not blessed with much weaponry. The small heterodontosaurs had a set of tusklike teeth that could have been used for defense. The iguanodonts had impressive spikes for thumbs, and it has been suggested that they used these to stab an attacker when battling at close range.[2] The larger, bulkier forms of ornithopods, including tenontosaurs, iguanodonts, and hadrosaurs, had thick, heavy tails that could be swung with great force. Even without a club at the end, slapping a predator with a 1,000-pound (450-kilogram) "baseball bat" would have been an effective way to repel a pursuing meat eater.

Numbers. The social nature of ornithopods strongly suggests that they gained protection by staying in close-knit herds or groups. There is abundant trackway evidence that iguanodonts and hadrosaurs moved in herds.[3] Jack Horner estimated one herd of *Maiasaura* to include as many as 10,000 individuals.[4] Herds of this size would have quickly stripped the local environment of available food, so it is likely that they traveled regularly, perhaps along annual migratory routes to and from nesting grounds.

Traveling together like this implies that the dinosaurs interacted and communicated in ways that would have increased their chances for survival. The hollow-crested duckbills were certainly capable of making loud and distinctive

Traveling together in large groups protected duckbills from predators.

sounds. Perhaps they used sound as a means to warn others of approaching danger or to cry for help.

Ornithopods such as hadrosaurs also took advantage of their great numbers when they were nesting. The nests were spaced closely enough so that adult members of the herd could stay with their eggs and babies. How remarkable it must have been to see a duckbill nesting site that stretched as far as the eye could see. Those members of the group that would have been in most danger from predators would have been the ones nesting around the outside border of the site and any that chose to wander off from the group. It is likely that the small, helpless ornithopod young were the most prized target of the small predators that roamed the outskirts of the nesting range.

CHAPTER 9

EXTINCTION OF THE DINOSAURS

The last of the dinosaurs became extinct 65 million years ago. Some of the most numerous of all ornithopods, the duck-billed dinosaurs, were among the last to go. However, they did not disappear because they were evolutionary failures. Dinosaurs were one of the most successful forms of life ever to inhabit our planet. They ruled the earth for 160 million years. By comparison, humans and even our most distant relatives have been around for only about 4 million years.

Extinction is the irreversible elimination of an entire species of plant or animal. Once it occurs, there is no turning back. It is also a natural process. More than 99 percent of all the species of organisms that have ever lived are now extinct.[1]

Although the dinosaurs existed for so many millions of years, most species existed for only a few million years at a time, until they became extinct or evolved into "improved" versions that adapted to changes in the environment. So, to say that all the dinosaurs became extinct at the end of the Cretaceous Period is incorrect—most kinds of dinosaurs had already come and gone by then. There is no denying, however, that a mass extinction occurred at the end of the Cretaceous Period that wiped out about 65 to 70 percent of all animal life.[2] Even those groups of animals that survived—including frogs, lizards, turtles, salamanders, birds, insects, fish, crocodiles, alligators, and mammals—lost great numbers of their species.

Chief among the causes of animal extinction are environmental changes that affect their food supply or body chemistry (such as extreme temperatures), disease, and natural disasters (such as volcanic eruptions, earthquakes, and the changing surface of Earth). Extensive hunting by natural enemies may also contribute to extinction. Humans, for example, have hunted many animals such as the buffalo to extinction or near extinction.

Why did the last of the dinosaurs become extinct? This is a great mystery of science.

The death of the dinosaurs is difficult to explain because dinosaurs were part of a strangely selective extinction event. Any suitable explanation must account for the disappearance of dinosaurs as well as flying reptiles, reptiles that swam in the oceans, and ammonites and other sea creatures, including some types of clams, mollusks, and plankton. It must also explain why so many other types of animals continued to thrive after that event.

Theories of Dinosaur Extinction

THEORY	TYPE OF THEORY	PROBLEMS WITH THE THEORY
The Big Rumble ↵moke and dust spewed by mass ↵olcanic eruptions shrouded the ↵rth in darkness, killing plants, ↵oisoning the air and water, and ↵using the climate to cool.	Gradual	Does not explain why other land- and ocean-dwelling animals survived.
Shifting Continents ↵lanetary cooling caused by ↵hifting continents and changes ↵o the earth's oceans. Water ↵etween the land masses would ↵ave cooled the air and caused ↵ind.	Gradual	This happened very slowly. Why couldn't dinosaurs and marine reptiles have adapted to the climate change or moved to warmer climates?
Pesky Mammals ↵New mammals stole and ate ↵inosaur eggs.	Gradual	Does not explain why some sea life became extinct or why other egg-laying land animals such as snakes and lizards survived. Also, small mammals coexisted with dinosaurs for many millions of year without this happening.
Flower Poisoning ↵owers first appeared during ↵e Cretaceous Period. Were ↵inosaurs unable to adapt to ↵e chemical makeup of this ↵ew source of food?	Gradual	Plant-eating dinosaurs actually increased in diversity and numbers during the rise of the flowering plants.
ombardment from Space ↵mpact by an asteroid or comet ↵nrouded the earth in darkness ↵om debris thrown into the ↵tmosphere and may have poisoned the air. Plants died and ↵he climate cooled.	Sudden	Does not explain the survival of some land reptiles, mammals, birds, amphibians, and plants, or why certain ocean life perished but not others.
Supernova ↵xplosion of a nearby star bathed ↵he earth in deadly cosmic rays.	Sudden	Why did some life-forms die and not others?

Extinction Theories

Paleontologists disagree on the causes of dinosaur extinction and the length of time it took for this mass dying to occur. There are many theories about what happened. They come in two basic varieties: gradual causes and sudden causes.

Gradual causes would have required millions of years of change. Some possible gradual causes include global climate changes (warming or cooling), volcanic action, shifting continents, overpopulation, poisoning by flowering plants, and the appearance of egg-stealing mammals.

Sudden or catastrophic causes would have taken no longer than a few years to wipe out the dinosaurs. Popular theories for a rapid extinction include disease and the collision of an asteroid or comet with Earth.

So far, no single extinction theory can fully explain the great dying at the end of the age of dinosaurs. Evidence has been mounting in favor of the asteroid theory. But a collision with an asteroid may have been only the final blow in a gradual extinction that had been mounting for many years. The asteroid theory also fails to explain why the extinction was so selective. Why did marine reptiles die but most fish survive? Why did dinosaurs of all sizes disappear but birds continue to thrive? There are still many questions to answer before scientists fully understand this great mystery.

CHAPTER 10

MAJOR ORNITHOPOD DISCOVERIES

This chapter summarizes the major discoveries of the plant-eating dinosaurs collectively known as the ornithopods. It chronicles the most important and complete specimens of duckbills, iguanodonts, and other ornithopods discovered, where they were found, and the people who identified them.

✦ ✦ ✦

1822 (England)—The term *dinosaur* had not yet been coined. A dinosaur fossil was found consisting of teeth that were correctly described for the first time as being from a large, unique reptilian creature that had become extinct. The dinosaur was *Iguanodon* ("iguana tooth"), a large plant eater. While physician and amateur geologist **Gideon Mantell** is credited with writing the memoir announcing the discovery, his wife **Mary**

Ann Mantell is often credited with having discovered the fossil tooth along a roadside in Lewes and recognizing its value. Gideon formally named the creature *Iguanodon* in 1825.

✦ ✦ ✦

1824 (England)—Professor **William Buckland** wrote the first scientific description of a dinosaur when he wrote about the carnivore *Megalosaurus* ("great lizard").

✦ ✦ ✦

1842 (England)—British anatomist **Richard Owen**, having recognized the differences between *Iguanodon, Megalosaurus,* and other large, extinct saurians described by that time, created the term *Dinosauria* ("terrible lizards") as a means for scientifically classifying the unique animals. This is the origin of the word *dinosaur.*

✦ ✦ ✦

1856 (United States)—**Joseph Leidy**, an anatomist and paleontologist in Philadelphia, described the first four dinosaurs positively identified in America. The specimens consisted only of teeth that were recovered by an expedition led by **Ferdinand Vandiveer Hayden** into the Montana territory. But Leidy's keen diagnostic eye recognized the special nature of these specimens. Four dinosaurs were named: *Troodon, Trachodon* ("rough tooth"), *Palaeoscincus* ("ancient skink"), and *Deinodon* ("terror tooth"). *Trachodon* was a duck-billed dinosaur.

✦ ✦ ✦

1858 (United States)—The bones of the most complete dinosaur discovered by this time in America were excavated from a marl pit on a private farm in Haddonfield, New Jersey. Named *Hadrosaurus* ("bulky lizard") by **Joseph Leidy**, the skeleton was about a third complete and belonged to a duck-billed dinosaur. Leidy was able to show that the dinosaur walked on two legs and was a plant eater. In 1868, *Hadrosaurus* became the first dinosaur skeleton mounted anywhere in the world when it went on display at the Academy of Natural Sciences in Philadelphia, Pennsylvania.

1869 (England)—The small two-legged plant-eating *Hypsilophodon* ("high-ridged tooth") was named by **Thomas Henry Huxley**. Found on the Isle of Wight, this small dinosaur measured only about 5 feet (1.5 meters) long. It was the first member discovered of the group of small- to medium-sized ornithopods collectively known as hypsilophodonts. *Hypsilophus*, after which this dinosaur was named, was a kind of iguana. Huxley named it after an iguana to suggest that it was similar to Mantell's *Iguanodon*.[1]

1878 (Belgium)—Workers in a coal mine in Bernissart discovered a rich deposit of *Iguanodon* bones deep in the earth. The skeletons were articulated, showing how the bones of the animals fit together. This answered many questions, including the position of the thumb spike, which Mantell had originally interpreted as being a nose horn. This unusual find remains one of the most valuable in the history of dinosaur science due to the number of specimens discovered of the same kind of dinosaur. As a result of this work, the Royal Museum in Brussels now displays eleven standing skeletons and twenty specimens mounted in their original rock slabs. Paleontologist **Louis Dollo** devoted most of his career to studying the fossils of Bernissart.

1883 (United States)—A remarkably complete specimen of a hadrosaur was described by **Edward Drinker Cope**. Found in South Dakota the previous year, it was the first good evidence for the head of these creatures. Cope originally named it *Diclonius* ("double sprout," referring to the teeth) in 1876, but it later became known as *Anatotitan* ("duck titan"). In his description, Cope mentioned the "double spoon-like bill" that made up the large plant eater's jaws. This was the origin of the term *duckbill*, which eventually became the popular name for all hadrosaurs.

1885 (United States)—*Camptosaurus*, a medium-sized two-legged plant eater, was discovered in Wyoming in 1879 and named by **Othniel Charles Marsh** in 1885. It is an ancestor of the iguanodonts.

1890 (United States)—One of the most primitive of hadrosaurs was uncovered in Kansas and described by **Othniel Charles Marsh**. Known as *Claosaurus* ("broken lizard"), the dinosaur is thought to be the bridge in the evolutionary gap between the earlier *Camptosaurus* ("bent lizard") and later hadrosaurs.

1894 (United States)—The small ornithopod *Dryosaurus* ("oak lizard") from the western United States was named by **Othniel Charles Marsh**. It was a small dinosaur, about 12 feet (3.7 meters) long, and resembled the hypsilophodonts in many ways except that it did not have any teeth at the front of its jaws.

1903 (Romania)—The skull of a primitive hadrosaur was discovered in Transylvania and identified by paleontologist **Baron Franz Nopcsa**. *Telmatosaurus* ("swamp lizard") was one of the few duck-billed dinosaurs to be found in Europe. Its primitive form suggests that it was an ancestor of North American hadrosaurs.

1908 (United States)—The **Sternberg** family of fossil collectors excavated one of the rarest dinosaur fossils of all—a large duck-billed dinosaur with large portions of its skin petrified over its body. Found in Wyoming, this dinosaur mummy of *Edmontosaurus* can be seen in the American Museum of Natural History in New York City.

1912 (Alberta, Canada)—The large duck-billed dinosaur *Saurolophus* ("crested saurian") was named by legendary fossil collector **Barnum Brown**. It had a bony spike running along the top of the skull, but it was not hollow like the crests later discovered in duckbills such as *Parasaurolophus*.

1914 (**Alberta, Canada**)—*Gryposaurus* ("hook-nosed lizard") was described by **Lawrence Lambe**. It was a large duck-billed dinosaur without a head crest. It had a spacious snout, after which it was named.

✦ ✦ ✦

1914 (**Alberta, Canada**)—**Barnum Brown** named *Corythosaurus* ("Corinthian helmet lizard") after the large fan-shaped crest on top of its head. It was a large duck-billed dinosaur.

✦ ✦ ✦

1916 (**Alberta, Canada**)—*Prosaurolophus* ("before crested saurian") was a large hadrosaur related to *Edmontosaurus*. Its name, given by **Barnum Brown**, suggested that this duck-billed dinosaur was probably the ancestor of another dinosaur named *Saurolophus*.

✦ ✦ ✦

1917 (**Alberta, Canada**)—Canadian paleontologist **Lawrence Lambe** described *Edmontosaurus* ("Edmonton lizard," after the Edmonton formation in Alberta, Canada). At 30 feet (9 meters) long, it was one of the largest known duck-billed dinosaurs. Several other duck-billed dinosaur discoveries were eventually renamed *Edmontosaurus*, including some specimens of *Claosaurus*.

✦ ✦ ✦

1922 (**Alberta, Canada**)—The duck-billed dinosaur *Parasaurolophus* ("near *Saurolophus*") was named by **William Arthur Parks**. This hadrosaur had the largest and most distinctive head crest of all the duckbills.

1923 (Alberta, Canada)—*Lambeosaurus* ("Lambe's lizard") was described by **William Arthur Parks** and named after fellow paleontologist **Lawrence Lambe**. *Lambeosaurus* was a moderate-sized hadrosaur with a paddle-shaped crest on its head.

✦ ✦ ✦

1933 (China)—The small hadrosaur *Bactrosaurus* ("staff lizard") was discovered in Asia and named by **Charles W. Gilmore** of the Smithsonian Institution. It was about 13 feet (4 meters) long. It was one of the earliest of the hadrosaurs.

✦ ✦ ✦

1958 (China)—*Tsintaosaurus* ("Tsingtao lizard," after the city of Tsingtao near where it was discovered) was named by **Chung Chien Young**. It was notable for the tall, slender bone rising up from between the eyes on top of its head.

✦ ✦ ✦

1962 (South Africa)—*Heterodontosaurus* ("different-toothed lizard") was named by **Alfred Crompton** and **Alan Charig**. The small, two-legged plant eater was one of the earliest ornithopods.

✦ ✦ ✦

1966 (China)—*Probactrosaurus* ("before staff lizard") was an iguanodont from the Late Cretaceous formations of Mongolia and may have been an ancestor of *Bactrosaurus*. It was named by Russian paleontologist **A. K. Rozhdestvensky**.

✦ ✦ ✦

1970 (United States)—*Tenontosaurus* ("tendon lizard") was named by **John Ostrom**. Originally discovered in Montana, its bones were found along with those of several *Deinonychus*, the meat-eating raptor. This suggests that *Deinonychus*, which was smaller than *Tenontosaurus*, may have attacked the 20-foot (6-meter) plant eater in packs. The name *Tenontosaurus* refers to the stiff bony tendons in its tail that helped keep it elevated and straight for balance. *Tenontosaurus* was a relative of the iguanodonts.

◆ ◆ ◆

1973 (China)—*Shantungosaurus* ("Shantung lizard," named after the location where it was found) was a large, flat-headed

Tenontosaurus builds a nest.

duck-billed dinosaur. It was named by **C. Hu**. The estimated length of this giant of the duckbills is 49 feet (15 meters), making it the largest of all known hadrosaurs.

✦ ✦ ✦

1975 (South Africa)—James A. Hopson named *Abrictosaurus* ("awake lizard"), a primitive ornithopod found in Late Triassic deposits. It was similar to *Heterodontosaurus.*

✦ ✦ ✦

1976 (Niger)—The unique sail-backed *Ouranosaurus* ("valiant lizard") was named by French paleontologist **Philippe Taquet**. This 23-foot- (7-meter-) long ornithopod is considered an iguanodont and a possible ancestor of the hadrosaurs.

✦ ✦ ✦

1978 (Lesotho)—A small, 3-foot- (90-centimeter) long primitive ornithopod was named *Lesothosaurus* ("Lesotho lizard") by **Peter M. Galton** after the African country in which it was found. It is one of the earliest known dinosaurs with an ornithischian hip.

✦ ✦ ✦

1979 (United States)—John "Jack" **Horner** and **Robert Makela** named *Maiasaura* ("good-mother lizard"), a 30-foot- (9-meter-) long duck-billed dinosaur found in Montana. The dinosaur was found with remains of eggs, nests, and hatchling *Maiasaura*, leading to many ideas related to parental care and social behavior of these dinosaurs.

1981 (Australia)—*Muttaburrasaurus* ("Muttaburra lizard"), an iguanodont, was named by **Alan Bartholomai** and **Ralph E. Molnar**.

✦ ✦ ✦

1988 (United States)—*Orodromeus* ("mountain runner"), an 8-foot- (2.4-meter-) long hypsilophodont, was named by **John "Jack" Horner** and **David B. Weishampel**.

✦ ✦ ✦

1990 (China)—*Agilisaurus* ("agile lizard"), a small and primitive ornithopod, was named by Chinese paleontologist **Peng Guangzhao**.

✦ ✦ ✦

1998 (United States)—**James Kirkland** named *Eolambia* ("dawn lambeosaurine"), a primitive, crestless duck-billed dinosaur found in Utah.

Eolambia

1998 (United States)—*Protohadros* ("first hadrosaur") was named by **Jason Head**. This iguanodont shares many characteristics of the early hadrosaurs.

✦ ✦ ✦

1998 (Mongolia)—A large iguanodont measuring about 23 to 26 feet (7 to 8 meters) long was named *Altirhinus* ("high snout") by **David Norman**. It had an expanded nasal cavity and more replacement teeth than most iguanodonts.

✦ ✦ ✦

1998 (Argentina)—The discovery of *Notohypsilophodon* in the Late Cretaceous deposits of Chubut Province, Argentina, extended the known geographic range of these dinosaurs to South America. It was named by **Rubén Martínez**.

✦ ✦ ✦

1999 (Argentina)—*Anabisetia*, a small ornithopod, was named by Argentine paleontologists **Rodolfo Coria** and **J. Calvo**.

✦ ✦ ✦

1999 (Niger)—The fossils of a large, heavy iguanodont that resembled in some ways a giant ground sloth were named *Lurdusaurus* ("heavy lizard") by **Philippe Taquet** and **Dale Russell**. The bones were originally found in 1965 and given the unofficial name of *Gravisaurus*. It must have been a ponderous animal with a heavy body that nearly touched the ground when it walked on all fours with its short legs. The nearly complete skeleton is about 30 feet (9 meters) long and has many unmistakable iguanodont features, including large thumb spikes. However, its size and general body shape are unique among the ornithopods.

CURRENTLY KNOWN ORNITHOPODS

The list below includes the genus names of currently known and scientifically accepted ornithopods. Each genus name is followed by the name(s) of the paleontologist(s) who described the animal in print and the year in which it was named.

Camptosaurs
Camptosaurus—Marsh, 1885

Dryosaurs
Dryosaurus—Marsh, 1894
Valdosaurus—Galton, 1977

Hadrosaurs
Anasazisaurus—Hunt and Lucas, 1993
Anatotitan—Chapman and Brett-Surman, 1990
Aralosaurus—Rozhdestvensky, 1968
Bactrosaurus—Gilmore, 1933
Brachylophosaurus—Sternberg, 1953
Claosaurus—Marsh, 1890
Corythosaurus—Brown, 1914
Edmontosaurus—Lambe, 1920
Eolambia—Kirkland, 1998
Gilmoreosaurus—Brett-Surman, 1979
Gryposaurus—Lambe, 1914
Hadrosaurus—Leidy, 1858
Hypacrosaurus—Brown, 1913
Kritosaurus—Brown, 1910
Lambeosaurus—Parks, 1923
Lophorhothon—Langston, 1960

Maiasaura—Horner and Makela, 1979
Naashoibitosaurus—Hunt and Lucas, 1993
Parasaurolophus—Parks, 1922
Prosaurolophus—Brown, 1916
Saurolophus—Brown, 1912
Secernosaurus—Brett-Surman, 1979
Shantungosaurus—Hu, 1973
Tanius—Wiman, 1929
Telmatosaurus—Nopcsa, 1903
Tsintaosaurus—Young, 1958

Heterodontosaurs
Abrictosaurus—Hopson, 1975
Heterodontosaurus—Crompton and Charig, 1962
Lycorhinus—Haughton, 1924

Hypsilophodonts
Agilisaurus—Peng, 1990
Atlascopcosaurus—Rich and Rich, 1989
Drinker—Bakker, Galton, Siegwarth, and Filla, 1992
Fulgurotherium—Huene, 1932
Gongbusaurus—Dong, Zhou, and Zhang, 1983
Hypsilophodon—Huxley, 1869
Leaellynasaura—Rich and Rich, 1989
Notohypsilophodon—Martínez, 1998
Orodromeus—Horner and Weishampel, 1988
Othnielia—Galton, 1977
Parksosaurus—Sternberg, 1937
Qantassaurus—Rich and Vickers-Rich, 1999
Thescelosaurus—Gilmore, 1913
Yandusaurus—He, 1979
Zephyrosaurus—Sues, 1980

Iguanodonts
Altirhinus—Norman, 1998

Anabisetia—Coria and Calvo, 1999
Callovosaurus—Galton, 1980
Craspedodon—Dollo, 1883
Iguanodon—Mantell, 1825
Lurdusaurus—Taquet and Russell, 1999
Ouranosaurus—Taquet, 1976
Probactrosaurus—Rozhdestvensky, 1966
Protohadros—Head, 1998
Rhabdodon—Matheron, 1869

Others
Lesothosaurus—Galton, 1978
Muttaburrasaurus—Bartholomai and Molnar, 1981
Tenontosaurus—Ostrom, 1970

CHAPTER NOTES

Chapter 1. Dinosaurs Defined

1. Peter Dodson and Susan D. Dawson, "Making the Fossil Record of Dinosaurs," *Modern Geology*, vol. 16, 1991, p. 13.

Chapter 2. Origins and Evolution

1. David B. Weishampel, Peter Dodson, and Halszka Osmólska, eds., *The Dinosauria* (Berkeley, Calif.: University of California Press, 1990), p. 11.

2. Paul Sereno, "The Evolution of Dinosaurs," *Science*, June 25, 1999, vol. 284, p. 2137.

3. Ibid.

4. Ibid.

Chapter 4. Anatomy

1. David Norman, *The Illustrated Encyclopedia of Dinosaurs* (London: Salamander Books Ltd., 1985), p. 101.

2. Ibid., p. 31.

3. Thom Holmes, "All About Hadrosaur Crests," *Dino Times*, vol. 7, no. 7, July 1997, pp. 4–5.

4. Thom Holmes, "Singing a Chorus for *Parasaurolophus*," *Dino Times*, vol. 7, no. 7, July 1997, pp. 1, 3.

Chapter 5. Physiology

1. Philip J. Currie and Kevin Padian, eds., *The Encyclopedia of Dinosaurs* (San Diego, Calif.: Academic Press, 1997), p. 371.

2. David E. Fastovsky and David B. Weishampel, *The Evolution and Extinction of the Dinosaurs* (Cambridge, England: Cambridge University Press, 1996), p. 339.

3. David Norman, *The Illustrated Encyclopedia of Dinosaurs* (London: Salamander Books Ltd., 1985), p. 106.

4. Ibid., p. 127; David B. Weishampel, Peter Dodson, and Halszka Osmólska, eds., *The Dinosauria* (Berkeley, Calif.: University of California Press, 1990), p. 547.

5. David Norman, *Dinosaur!* (New York: Prentice Hall, 1991), p. 166.

6. John R. Horner and James Gorman, *Digging Dinosaurs* (New York: Workman, 1988), pp. 84–85.

7. Fastovsky and Weishampel, based on Fig. 14.11, p. 346.

8. Dale A. Russell, *An Odyssey in Time* (Toronto: University of Toronto Press, 1989), p. 150.

9. Anusuya Chinsamy, "Ontogenetic Changes in the Bone Histology of the Late Jurassic Ornithopod *Dryosaurus letowvorbecki,*" *Journal of Vertebrate Paleontology,* 1995, vol. 15, pp. 96–104.

10. Philip J. Currie and Kevin Padian, eds., *The Encyclopedia of Dinosaurs* (San Diego, Calif.: Academic Press, 1997), p. 282.

11. Kenneth Carpenter, Karl F. Hirsch, and John R. Horner, eds., *Dinosaur Eggs and Babies* (Cambridge, England: Cambridge University Press, 1994), pp. 312–336.

12. James O. Farlow and Michael K. Brett-Surman, eds., *The Complete Dinosaur* (Bloomington, Ind.: Indiana University Press, 1997), pp. 499–501.

13. Edwin H. Colbert, R. B. Cowles, and C. M. Bogert, "Temperature Tolerances in the American Alligator and their Bearing on the Habits, Evolution, and Extinction of the Dinosaurs." *American Museum of Natural History Bulletin 86,* 1946, pp. 327–374.

14. Martin Lockley, *Tracking Dinosaurs* (Cambridge: Cambridge University Press, 1991), pp. 71–82.

15. R. McNeill Alexander, *Dynamics of Dinosaurs & Other Extinct Giants* (New York: Columbia University Press, 1989), p. 43.

16. Ibid., pp. 40–41.

17. Lockley, p. 63.

18. Alexander, p. 40; Richard Anthony Thulborn, "Estimated Speed of a Giant Bipedal Dinosaur," *Nature*, 1981, no. 292, pp. 273–274.

19. Fastovsky and Weishampel, p. 439.

20. Weishampel, Dodson, and Osmólska, p. 495.

21. Weishampel, Dodson, and Osmólska, pp. 501–502.

22. Peter Dodson, "Taxonomic Implications of Relative Growth in Lambeosaurine Hadrosaurs," *Systematics of Zoology*, 1975, vol. 24, pp. 37–54.

Chapter 6. Eggs and Babies

1. Based on Kenneth Carpenter, Karl F. Hirsch, and John R. Horner, eds., *Dinosaur Eggs and Babies* (Cambridge, England: Cambridge University Press, 1994), pp. 15–30.

2. John R. Horner and James Gorman, *Digging Dinosaurs* (New York: Workman, 1988), p. 108.

3. Carpenter, Hirsch, and Horner, p. 42.

4. Ibid., p. 235.

5. David E. Fastovsky and David B. Weishampel, *The Evolution and Extinction of the Dinosaurs* (Cambridge, England: Cambridge University Press, 1996), p. 221.

6. Carpenter, Hirsch, and Horner, p. 322.

7. Horner and Gorman, p. 104.

8. Ibid., p. 128.

9. Ibid., p. 104.

Chapter 7. Feeding Habits and Adaptations

1. John R. Horner and James Gorman, *Digging Dinosaurs* (New York: Workman, 1988), pp. 78–79.

2. David E. Fastovsky and David B. Weishampel, *The Evolution and Extinction of the Dinosaurs* (Cambridge, England: Cambridge University Press, 1996), p. 213.

3. James O. Farlow and Michael K. Brett-Surman, eds., *The Complete Dinosaur* (Bloomington, Ind.: Indiana University Press, 1997), pp. 354–360.

4. Ibid., p. 359.

5. Joseph Wallace, *The American Museum of Natural History's Book of Dinosaurs and Other Ancient Creatures* (New York: Simon and Schuster, 1994), p. 101; Fastovsky and Weishampel, p. 213.

6. Farlow and Brett-Surman, p. 379.

7. Based on Debbie Ciszek, "Asian Elephant," *Animal Diversity Web* (University of Michigan), September 5, 1997, <http://animaldiversity.ummz.umich.edu/index.html> (February 5, 2000).

Chapter 8. Ornithopod Defenses

1. David Norman, *The Illustrated Encyclopedia of Dinosaurs* (London: Salamander Books Ltd., 1985), p. 61.

2. Ibid., p. 114.

3. Martin Lockley and Adrian Hunt, *Dinosaur Tracks* (New York: Columbia University Press, 1995), pp. 181–211.

4. John R. Horner and James Gorman, *Digging Dinosaurs* (New York: Workman, 1988), p. 128.

Chapter 9. Extinction of the Dinosaurs

1. David M. Raup, *Extinction: Bad Genes or Bad Luck* (New York: W. W. Norton, 1991), pp. 3–4.

2. Ibid., p. 71.

Chapter 10. Major Ornithopod Discoveries

1. Ben Creisler, "Dinosauria Translation and Pronunciation Guide," Revised October 18, 1999, <www.dinosauria.com/dml/names/dinosi.htm>.

GLOSSARY

angiosperms—The flowering plants, the last of the major plant groups to evolve.

archosaur—The group of reptiles that included the thecodonts (extinct), crocodiles (living and extinct); pterosaurs (extinct flying reptiles), and dinosaurs (extinct).

bilateral symmetry—A feature of vertebrate body design in which one side of the body is a mirror image of the other.

bipedal—Walking on two legs.

braincase—The internal portion of the skull that encloses and protects the brain.

carnivore—A meat-eating creature.

cast—To make an exact replica of the original using a mold.

caudal—Pertaining to the tail.

cervical—Pertaining to the neck.

chordate—Animals with backbones, including those with the precursor of the backbone called the notochord.

classification—A traditional system of classifying organisms based on their similarities in form. The hierarchy of this classification method is: kingdom, phylum, class, order, family, genus, species.

coprolite—Fossilized animal dung.

Cretaceous Period—The third and final major time division (144 to 65 million years ago) of the Mesozoic Era. The end of the age of dinosaurs.

duck-billed dinosaur—A popular name for all members of the Hadrosauridae family of ornithopod dinosaurs.

ectotherms—Cold-blooded animals whose body temperature is affected by the temperature of their environment and their behavior. They may actually become warmer than the air temperature while basking in full sunlight. Modern ectotherms include most fish, reptiles, and amphibians.

endotherms—Warm-blooded animals that generate their own body heat internally. They have a constant body temperature no matter what the temperature of their surroundings. Modern endotherms include mammals, birds, and some fish.

evolution—The pattern of change through time of living organisms.

extinction—The irreversible elimination of an entire species of plant or animal.

gymnosperms—Primitive seed plants found in two groups, the conifers and the cycads.

hadrosaur—The name given collectively to all duck-billed dinosaurs, after the first famous duckbill discovered, *Hadrosaurus*.

head crest—A bony or hollow structure on top of the head of a duck-billed dinosaur. The hollow forms were connected to the nose and were probably used to create sound and to let off excessive heat in the head.

herbivore—A plant-eating creature.

iguanodont—A member of the group of ornithopod dinosaurs that includes *Iguanodon*.

ilium—The upper bone of the hip, which attaches the pelvis to the backbone.

ischium—The more rearward of the lower bones of the hip.

Jurassic Period—The second of the three major time divisions (208 to 144 million years ago) of the Mesozoic Era.

manus—The hand or forefoot.

Mesozoic Era—The time of the dinosaurs (245 to 65 million years ago).

mosasaur—A fish-eating marine reptile with a deep, flat-sided tail. It was related to lizards, not dinosaurs.

nares—The openings of the nose.

olfactory—Pertaining to the sense of smell.

optic—Pertaining to vision.

orbit—The eye socket.

Ornithischia—One of two groups of dinosaurs based on hip structure. Ornithischians had a hip with a backward-pointing pubis bone.

ornithopods—A group of two-footed plant-eating ornithischian dinosaurs.

paleontologist—A scientist who studies life-forms of the geologic past, especially through the analysis of plant and animal fossils.

pelvis—The hipbones.

pes—The hindfoot.

plesiosaur—Marine reptiles of the Mesozoic Era that had a squat body, paddles as limbs, and either a long neck and small head or a short neck and big head.

predator—A creature that kills other creatures for food.

pteridophytes—Early primitive plants, including ferns, horsetails, and club mosses.

pterosaur—A flying reptile that lived during the Mesozoic Era.

pubis—The more forward of the lower bones of the hip.

quadrupedal—Walking on four legs.

raptor—Popular nickname for any member of the group of dromaeosaur theropods. Raptors are noted for the large retractable killing claw on the second toe of each foot.

Saurischia—One of two groups of dinosaurs based on hip structure. Saurischians had a hip with a forward-pointing pubis bone.

sauropod—Large plant-eating saurischian dinosaurs with long necks and long tails.

scapula—The shoulder blade.

sexual dimorphism—Differences in size, shape, physiology, and behavior between males and females of the same kind of animal.

thecodonts—One of the groups of reptiles that lived during the Triassic Period. The first meat-eating dinosaurs may have had their roots in the small bipedal thecodonts, some of the first reptiles to run on two legs.

theropod—A group of saurischian dinosaurs, all of which ate meat and walked on two legs.

tibia—The larger of the two bones in the lower leg; the other is the fibula.

Triassic Period—The first of the three major time divisions (245 to 208 million years ago) of the Mesozoic Era.

ulna—One of the two bones of the forearm; the other is the radius.

vertebra—A bone of the neck, spine, or tail.

vertebrate—Any animal that has a backbone (spine).

FURTHER READING

Even though there have been hundreds of books about dinosaurs published, reputable dinosaur books are hard to find. Listed here are some of the author's favorites. They range from the examination of individual kinds of dinosaurs to several encyclopedic volumes covering a wide range of dinosaur-related topics. A number of history books are included in the list as well to help those who are interested in the lives and times of paleontologists.

Bakker, Robert T. *The Dinosaur Heresies.* New York: William Morrow and Company, 1986.
This highly entertaining and colorful account of the days and lives of dinosaurs is both rich with scientific fact and speculation. Bakker provides his own marvelous and lively illustrations.

Colbert, Edwin H. *The Great Dinosaur Hunters and Their Discoveries.* New York: Dover Publications, 1984.
A classic book about the history of dinosaur discovery from the early nineteenth century to arctic explorations in the 1960s.

Dixon, Dougal, Barry Cox, R. J. G. Savage, and Brian Gardiner. *The Macmillan Illustrated Encyclopedia of Dinosaurs and Other Prehistoric Animals.* New York: Macmillan, 1988.
An overview of dinosaurs and other fossil vertebrates with easy-reference timelines throughout.

Farlow, James O., and Michael K. Brett-Surman, eds. *The Complete Dinosaur*. Bloomington, Ind.: Indiana University Press, 1997.
A comprehensive encyclopedia arranged by topics such as The Discovery of Dinosaurs, The Study of Dinosaurs, and Biology of the Dinosaurs. Contributions are by leading experts in the field.

Gallagher, William B. *When Dinosaurs Roamed New Jersey*. New Brunswick, N.J.: Rutgers University Press, 1997.
Prior to the widespread discovery of dinosaurs in the North American West, New Jersey was the mecca of dinosaur science on this continent. Paleontologist William Gallagher is still searching for dinosaurs in New Jersey and provides a lively and accessible account of dinosaurs and other important fossils found in the Garden State.

Holmes, Thom. *Fossil Feud: The Rivalry of the First American Dinosaur Hunters*. Parsippany, N.J.: Julian Messner, 1998.
The true story of two rival nineteenth-century American dinosaur scientists, Edward Drinker Cope of Philadelphia, Pennsylvania, and Othniel Charles Marsh of New Haven, Connecticut. Their bitter rivalry to find the most dinosaurs ignited dinosaur science in the latter half of the 1800s.

Horner, John R., and James Gorman. *Digging Dinosaurs*. New York, Workman, 1988.
This personal account of the discovery of duck-billed dinosaur eggs and nests by John "Jack" Horner highlights Horner's fossil evidence for dinosaur behavior.

Horner, John R., and James Gorman. *Maia, A Dinosaur Grows Up*. Bozeman, Mont.: Museum of the Rockies, Montana State University, 1985.
Written with paleontologist John "Jack" Horner, this book for young people fictionalizes the lives of the duck-billed dinosaurs known as Maiasaura based on fossil evidence from Montana.

Norell, Mark A., Eugene S. Gaffney, and Lowell Dingus. *Discovering Dinosaurs*. New York: Alfred A. Knopf, 1995.
Excellent question-and-answer book from the American Museum of Natural History in New York City, home of the world's largest collection of dinosaur fossils.

Norman, David. *The Illustrated Encyclopedia of Dinosaurs*. London: Salamander Books, 1985.
Richly illustrated and comprehensive encyclopedia for all ages.

Russell, Dale A. *The Dinosaurs of North America: An Odyssey in Time*. Minocqua, Wisc.: NorthWord Press, 1989.
An elegant examination of dinosaurs and the world they lived in, richly illustrated with contemporary photographs of dinosaur fossil sites. It is one of the best books available that describes the environment of the dinosaurs.

Spalding, David A. *Dinosaur Hunters*. Rocklin, Calif.: Prima Publishing, 1993.
The history of dinosaur science as seen through the work of its most famous contributors. This book is a good complement to Colbert's The Great Dinosaur Hunters and Their Discoveries *and covers many developments since Colbert's history in 1968.*

Sternberg, Charles H. *Life of a Fossil Hunter.* New York: Dover, 1990.

A reprint of the original 1909 memoir by one of paleontology's most famous fossil collectors. Sternberg worked for both Cope and Marsh during his long and illustrious career.

Weishampel, David B., and Luther Young. *Dinosaurs of the East Coast.* Baltimore, Md.: Johns Hopkins University Press, 1996.

The history of dinosaur discovery in the eastern half of North America is explored by this fascinating book combining science, history, and the results of new research into North America's dinosaur heritage.

Internet Addresses

American Museum of Natural History. *Fossil Halls.* n.d. <http:// www.amnh.org/exhibitions/Fossil_Halls/index.html>.

Denver Museum of Nature and Science. *Research: Cedar Mountain Dinosaur Project.* © 1998. <http://www.dmnh. org/cedarmnt/cmnt_17.htm>.

Discovery Communications, Inc. *Valley of the T. rex.* © 2000. <http://dsc.discovery.com/convergence/trex/trex.html>.

Jacobson, Russ. *Dino Russ's Lair: Dinosaur and Vertebrate Paleontology Information.* July 25, 2000. <http://www. isgs.uiuc.edu/dinos/dinos_home.html>.

National Geographic Society. *Dinosaur Eggs.* © 1996. <http:// www.nationalgeographic.com/dinoeggs/>.

The Natural History Museum, London. *Dinosaur Data Files.* © 1994–2000. <http://www.nhm.ac.uk/education/online/ dinosaur_data_files.html>.

Scotese, Christopher R. *Paleomap Project.* August 8, 2000. <http://www.scotese.com>.

Summer, Edward. *The Dinosaur Interplanetary Gazette.* April 22, 2000. <http://www.dinosaur.org/frontpage.html>.

Tyrrell Museum of Palaeontology, Alberta. *Dinosaur Hall.* © 1995–1997. <http://www.tyrrellmuseum.com/tour/dinohall.html>.

University of Bristol. *Dinobase.* n.d. <http://palaeo.gly.bris.ac.uk/dinobase/dinopage.html>.

University of California, Berkeley, Museum of Paleontology. *The Dinosauria: Truth Is Stranger Than Fiction.* © 1994–2000. <http://www.ucmp.berkeley.edu/diapsids/dinosaur.html>.

INDEX

ACCELERATED READER

READING LEVEL:___8.5___

POINTS:___3.0___